Orthodoxy and Heterodoxy

Orthodoxy and Heterodoxy

A Miscellany of Articles on Theology and Ethics

William G.T. Shedd

Solid Ground Christian Books
Birmingham, Alabama USA

Solid Ground Christian Books
715 Oak Grove Road
Homewood AL 35209
205-443-0311
solid-ground-books.com

ORTHODOXY AND HETERODOXY
A Miscellany of Articles on Theology and Ethics

William G.T. Shedd (1820-1894)

Solid Ground Christian Classic Reprints

Taken from 1893 edition by Charles Scribner's Sons, New York

Cover design by Borgo Design.
Contact them at borgogirl@bellsouth.net

ISBN 1-59925-098-5

PREFACE

This Miscellany is composed of articles, some of which were written for special occasions, and some for the religious journals. While having this temporary reference, they relate to principles in theology and ethics which are eternal, and are vehemently opposed in the standing conflict between orthodoxy and heterodoxy. For neither of these is a new thing. Both run parallel with each other in this apostate world, from the beginning. The history of mankind is the history of the contest between truth and error. Unfallen Adam was confronted with fallen Satan. When God incarnate appeared, the Tempter met him in the wilderness. The holy supernaturalism of the kingdom of Christ was beset by the demoniacal supernaturalism of the kingdom of evil in "signs and lying wonders;" and the Man of Sorrows, through his whole life of benevolence and love, was obstructed by "the powers of darkness." The regenerate church, from the first, has found an obstinate antagonist in the unregenerate world. Each kingdom has had its fluctuations, but truth steadily grows stronger, and evil weaker, in the lapse of time.

Orthodoxy is embodied in the dogmatic systems of ancient, mediæval, and modern Christendom, which present a massive body of Biblical truth against which in every generation the antagonistic theories of the heterodox strike in vain. And there is little originality, in the sense of new discovery, upon either side. The conservative only restates the old faith. The radical only revamps the old error. Each draws from his predecessors the best part of his defence, or of his attack. There is nothing new in the orthodoxy of to-day; and nothing new in the newest heterodoxy. A scholar versed in ancient learning can trace both alike in the antagonisms of the past. Speaking generally, the orthodox respects and cultivates systematic theology; the heterodox contemns and vilifies it. The former maintains the carefully stated creeds of the evangelical denominations; the latter seeks to revise, relax, and nullify them. Orthodoxy defines Christianity to be an exclusive religion, distinct from all others, and intended to convert them; heterodoxy explains it to be a conglomerate of all religions, and destined to be merged and lost in them.

This volume is *polemic* in the technical sense of the term. Its aim is to defend the historical faith, and to attack the contrary. Doctrines and not persons are in the writer's view; and respecting these his statements are explicit and unequivocal. One special object is to set forth and vindicate those stern and salutary phases of revealed truth which the Lord of heaven and earth had in mind when he said: "Think not that I am come to send peace on earth; I am not come to send peace but a sword. I am come to send fire on earth." Matt. 10 : 34 ; Luke 12 : 49. This is an aspect of Jesus Christ which is studiously concealed in the existing onset of licence upon law, of heterodoxy upon orthodoxy. A healthy and vigorous state of religion, in all the churches, requires that this solemn and retributive attitude of incarnate God towards error and unbelief emerge again into luminous view, as it always has in the heroic and powerful ages of Christianity. All true religion represents the Supreme Being as ethically strict and holy, and all false religion as ethically easy and indulgent. The revelation which God made to Moses, when he established the Jewish church, announced both his "goodness" and his "severity" (Rom. 11 : 22) in combination. On the entrance of the Israelites into the promised land, Jehovah proclaimed both his mercy and his justice, in the blessings of Gerazim and the curses of Ebal. And when the second Person of the Trinity laid the legal foundations of the Christian church in his Sermon on the Mount, the Divine emotions towards righteousness and unrighteousness were reaffirmed. The two explain each other, and one is unintelligible without the other. The mercy of God is a cheap and unmeaning thing for the self-indulgent man who "thinks his Maker to be altogether such an one as himself." The love of God needs the foil of the wrath of God to set it off, and make it bright and effulgent. A foil is a leaf of metal placed under jewels to increase their brilliancy. If taken away, they are dimmed. A generation that denies or ignores the Divine displeasure against wrong doctrine and wrong living, cannot have a vivid sense of the Divine compassion. No man knows how absolutely infinite is the mercy of God, unless he first perceives what God might in justice do to him. The dazzling light of the Heavenly Pity is flashed only from the background of the Heavenly Purity.

Books of this tenor are needed at the present juncture. Heterodoxy is, perhaps, more violent and resolute at the close of this century than ever before, and it is favored by the comparative apathy of orthodoxy. In the previous conflicts, the Church has stood alone by itself, holding its creed determinedly, and fighting its foe unflinchingly. There has been no admixture of truth and error. Now, the danger is that the orthodox shall weaken, and tolerate, and yield. The former sharp distinction between the church and the world, the regenerate and the unregenerate, is blunted, and a considerable membership has entered the evangelical churches, which cannot be relied upon to defend strong views and statements of doctrine. What is needed is the concentrated and combined energy of the really orthodox in all denominations, to preserve their historical creeds, and maintain their ancient discipline.

The last four of the articles in the volume differ from the others in being political in their bearing. The concluding one, on "The Union and the War," presents the writer's views of the Federal Union, of Slavery and Secession, of the right of Revolution in a Democracy, and of the true type of statesmanship under the American Constitution.

NEW YORK, October, 1893.

CONTENTS

	PAGE
THEOLOGICAL INDEPENDENCE,	1
COURAGE IN THE MINISTRY,	24
INJUNCTIONS TO MINISTERS,	31
ONE TRUTH FOR ALL PULPITS,	43
DOCTRINAL PREACHING,	47
BONED PREACHING,	51
THE EVILS OF PULPIT NOTORIETY,	55
OVERESTIMATED POPULARITY,	59
WIT AND HUMOR IN PREACHING,	64
THE CREDULITY OF INFIDELITY,	68
INFIDELITY SEEKS A SIGN FROM HEAVEN,	72
THE HASTY INFERENCES OF INFIDELITY,	79
STEREOTYPED ERRORS OF INFIDELITY,	83
THE EFFRONTERY OF INFIDELITY,	88
THE MEANNESS OF INFIDELITY,	93
THE CONNECTION BETWEEN INFIDELITY AND SENSUALITY,	97
THE INFIDEL PHYSICS,	101
MODERN APOCRYPHAL GOSPELS,	106
THE TWO VIEWS OF THE OLD TESTAMENT,	112
CONJECTURAL CRITICISM,	128
PSEUDO-HIGHER CRITICISM,	143
FLUCTUATIONS IN GERMAN THEOLOGY,	154
HUMAN ALTERATIONS OF THE FOURTH COMMANDMENT,	162
LIBERAL BIGOTRY,	167
"ORTHODOX DISBELIEF,"	174

	PAGE
"Orthodox Disbelief" (again),	178
Endless Punishment an Essential Doctrine of Christianity,	183
Hellphobia,	189
The Sinner at Rest,	193
All Religions not Equally Valuable,	198
Christianity alone is Able to Incline a Man,	207
The Reason why Sin should be Forgiven,	211
Advice to the Inquiring Sinner,	216
Vicarious Atonement and Philanthropy,	222
The Doctrine of Immortality,	226
The Certainty of Future Blessedness,	230
The Habit of Reading the Bible,	235
A Little Religion is a Dangerous Thing,	239
Not Wealth, but Competence,	243
Denominational Unity Undesirable,	247
An American Fault,	254
Political Fanaticism,	259
The Dangers of Office-holding,	263
The Union and the War,	267

THEOLOGICAL INDEPENDENCE

GENTLEMEN: In beginning a new year of theological study, it is natural to go to the Word of God for a word of instruction and of stimulus. The particular kind of instruction needed by both a teacher and a student is determined by the form and pressure of the time in which he lives. Special tendencies of the age call for special lessons. We are summoned to study theology in an apologetic age, rather than in a dogmatic one. The foundations of faith are now menaced. Men are denying the first principles of religion: the existence of God, the immortality of the soul, the reality of the distinction between right and wrong, the freedom of the human will, the certainty of endless reward and punishment. In this state of things, it commonly happens that those evangelical doctrines which presuppose these truths of natural religion are somewhat overlooked. In an age of speculative unbelief, it cannot be expected that dogmatic theology will attract so much atten-

[1] A Discourse delivered in Union Seminary.

tion as apologetic theology. The first period in doctrinal history was engaged with the defences of Christianity, and it was not until this effort was concluded that the ecclesiastical mind entered upon the discussion of the more recondite and vexing topics of the trinity, original sin, vicarious atonement, and predestination. For the last twenty years Christendom has been employed in refuting the arguments of atheists and materialists, and for this reason has devoted less attention to the scientific construction of Christian doctrine itself. In some quarters this has led to an undervaluation of strictly dogmatic statements; so that some good men are inclined to dispense with all but the more vague and general definitions of revealed truth. But this condition of things is temporary. When apologetics shall have once again, as in former periods, refuted and banished the popular unbelief, dogmatics will once again enlist the acumen and energy of the scientific mind. Meanwhile the Christian student and minister has a particular duty to perform in reference to this whole subject of scepticism: and it is, the duty of Theological Independence.

By this, I mean, not independence of divine authority and revelation, but of human opinion, human science, and human literature. The words of St. Paul (1 Cor. 4 : 3) should be the watchword and the battle-cry of the theologian: "With me it is a very small thing that I should be judged of you, or of man's judgment"; or, as the original text reads, "by a human day." To be judged by a "human day" is to be judged by the spirit of the age. The spirit of an age is reflected in its philosophy, science, literature, and art. Revelation is judged by a "human day," whenever it is interpreted by the shifting theories in human speculation, and the changing fashions in human taste and culture, instead of being interpreted by itself. St. Paul teaches that Revelation is self-consistent and self-explaining, and therefore will not submit to be made consistent with something that is not itself, or to be explained by it. Christian doctrine, he contends, should be an evolution out of inspired materials, not a manufacture out of uninspired. The apostle does not concede for a moment, that the Christian religion is the product of any of the human centuries, even the vaunted nineteenth, and that like such products it may be subjected to the test of varying and oftentimes contradictory systems of science and philosophy, and temporary schools of literature and art. He asserts the difference in kind between the spiritual and the natural, the revealed and the non-revealed, and affirms the superiority of the Christian religion not only to all other religions, but to all secular knowledge. "The foolishness of God is wiser than men." 1 Cor. 1 : 25. For this reason, he maintains that divine revelation is to criticise and judge the products of the human intellect, and that no product of the human intellect is to criticise and judge divine revelation. "He that is spiritual judgeth all things, yet he himself is judged of no man." 1 Cor. 2 : 15. According to St. Paul, divine revelation is higher than any "human day," than the spirit of any human age however enlightened and progressive, than the human mind itself. He echoes the words of St. John, "He that is of the earth is earthly, and speaketh of the earth: he that cometh from heaven is above all." John 3:31.

I purpose to direct your attention to the proper attitude of the theologian and preacher toward the secular spirit; that is, toward the intellectual movements and products of the time in which he lives.

The proper attitude is that of independence, because Christian theology is derived from an infallible source. If this fact can be established, and is conceded, it of course elevates this theology above all the natural operations of the human intellect. For no product of the human intellect can be more trustworthy than the human intellect itself. No physics or ethics can be more reliable than its author. The Darwinian theory of evolution can have as much infallibility as Darwin had, but no more. The Spencerian ethics can be as free from all error as the intellect that made it, but no more. The demand, therefore, that Christianity submit to be judged and criticised by human science and philosophy requires, in order to be consistent, that these latter claim infallibility. This is what Christianity does, when it subjects human science and philosophy to its criticism. The conflict between the Christian religion and science, if there be one, is ultimately a question as to which of the two is inerrant. One or the other must be, in order to be an arbiter over the other, and a court of last appeal.

I do not propose to prove that the Christian Scriptures are an infallible revelation from God, but shall assume that this has been proved. I am addressing those who believe that it has been proved by an argument to which, for variety, massiveness and strength, no other religion or system can show an equal or a parallel. For that the Christian religion has presented more proof, and stronger proof of infallibility than any system of human science has yet presented, can hardly be doubted. It is certainly more probable that Moses and the prophets were under a special divine influence, than that Hobbes and Spinoza were; more probable that Jesus Christ had immediate connection with God and the invisible world, than that Socrates and Confucius, and still less Boodha and Mohammed had. Comparing the influence which the Christian religion has exerted in the world, and the kind of effect it has produced, with that exerted and produced by any human system of religion or of science, it is certainly more credible that the former is from heaven than that the latter is.

Assuming, then, that there is such a thing as an infallible revelation from God, and that the theologian derives his system from it, I proceed to specify some particulars in respect to which he should be independent of what St. Paul denominates "a human day."

1. In the first place the theologian should be

independent of the *secular spirit* and of *popular opinion*, in the interpretation of Scripture, and the construction of a creed. The church must not go to the literary and scientific world in order to find the meaning of the Bible, but to the Bible itself. The theologian should not ask either the physicist or the belle-lettrist for a systematic construction of the doctrines of religion, but should formulate them for himself. There is just now need of warning upon this point. As in all ages the world is prone in practical morals to encroach upon the church, and strives to infuse its frivolity and fashions into it, so in this age an uncommon effort is being made by the votaries of culture to inject their views of religion into Christianity; in their phrase, to liberalize Christianity. They claim to occupy a position superior to that of the theologian for the formation of a religion that is suited to man in an advanced civilization, and insist that the church purge its creed of certain doctrines that offend their taste, or their sentiments. A different interpretation of Scripture from that of the church, and a milder creed, are required, they say, by an age so progressive and cultivated as the present one.

The so-called polite literature, in particular, is now the channel in which this claim is conveyed. The belle-lettrist, in the novel, the poem, and the essay, throws a silken gauze over all the serious and solemn features of Christianity, and contends that the traditional explanation of the words of Christ, whose authority he does not venture to discard altogether, is antiquated, and incompatible with human civilization and refinement. The holy teachings of the Redeemer concerning sin and punishment, the day of judgment and eternal death, are omitted, and "the grace of God" is converted into what the theorist calls a "sweet reasonableness," but what the apostle denominates "lasciviousness." This belle-lettrist theology is exerting a mischievous influence upon that younger class of educated persons who have not reached what Wordsworth denominates "the years that bring the philosophic mind," and gradually Christianity is being emptied of its life and force, and religion becomes a weak sentimentalism, or a despairing unbelief.

The duty and proper temper of the theologian and preacher in this state of things is that of independence. The question is not one of taste, but of eternal truth; not of the ornaments of life, genuine or counterfeit, elegant or tawdry, but of human destiny. We are far from undervaluing genuine literature or genuine science, in their proper place and connections. Neither of them has suffered at the hands, or under the influence of the Christian religion. Some of their finest products, like "Kepler's Laws," the "Divine Comedy," and the "Paradise Lost," have arisen under the more logical and severer forms of Christian truth. But the question for the theologian, we repeat, is neither literary nor scientific. It is religious. His first search must be for the mind of God in Revelation, not for the opinions of man in poetry, philosophy, science and art. Without, therefore, being diverted by the opinions of the scientist, or the belle-lettrist, as to what the Scriptures teach, or should teach, let him betake himself to the study of the Word, and find its real meaning for himself.

This line of remark holds good also in respect to the formulation of Scripture data into a creed. Indeed, it has even more force in this reference. In collating and combining the Biblical elements into a symbol for the use of a church, the theologian should be entirely independent of the secular spirit. The councils and assemblies that constructed those symbols that have guided and consolidated the great Christian communions that adopted them, were very little under the influence of "a human day." They thought themselves to be under the influence of the Holy Ghost, and there is reason to believe that they were. The statements of the Apostles' and Nicene Creeds, of the Augsburg, Heidelberg and Westminster confessions, were not derived from philosophy or literature, but from the unadulterated Revelation.

There are two errors made current by some literary men in this age, which, if adopted, interfere with the independence of the theologian, and bring him into bondage to the secular spirit and popular opinion. The first is, the separation of religion from theology; and the second, the notion that religion can exist and prosper without the science of religion, that is, without creed statements: for theological creeds are theological science.

This false view of the relation of religion to theology, and of the life to the creed, has become wide-spread. A clamorous demand of this "human day" is for a religiousness wholly disconnected from definite statements concerning either the character of God or man; concerning either sin or salvation. A considerable class of educated and literary men tell us that they can worship without a Biblical creed, and ask us to do the same. One bright Sunday morning Thomas Carlyle received a letter bringing the sad tidings of the death of John Sterling. "If on that day," said he, "I did no worship in the great cathedral of Immensity, surely the fault was my own." It is hazardous to state a man's creed for him. But probably no injustice is done to that impetuous and eccentric intellect, in asserting that the distinguishing doctrines of the Apostles' creed formed no part of his belief. He accepted the truths of deism: the divine existence, the reality of right and wrong, the immortality of the soul, future reward and punishment; but he rejected the truths of revelation: the trinity, the incarnation, the apostasy and the redemption. The "worship," whatever it was, which he rendered under the open sky, could not therefore have rested upon these tenets of Christendom. The "worship," whatever it was, could not have related to the Father, Son and Holy Ghost; could not have postulated the deity, miraculous birth and acts of Jesus Christ; could not have involved the confession of sin and its remission through expiation. That there was great awe, under the sense of the mystery of life and of death, and of the immensity of their relations, there can be no doubt. That a strong tide of mixed and tumultuous feeling flowed through the soul, investing man and the universe with deep solemnity, there can be no doubt. But this is religion divorced from theology; worship apart from the Christian gospel. It is an attempt to produce in the human soul that form of consciousness which man ought to have towards God, without adopting those views of God which have been revealed as a guide and test in this very case.

The theologian is bound to rise above this demand of the belle-lettrist, and assert both the necessity of Christian science and the independence of Christian science. Christianity must "keep state," to use the phrase of Howe, relying solely upon its own God-given power and resources. It was one of the merits of Schleiermacher, that he maintained that theology should stand alone. He refused to make it the slave of philosophy. For him it was an independent and a self-sustaining science. He would find its elements in the Christian consciousness, not in the secular; in the experience of the church, not of the world. It is indeed true that he was unsuccessful in carrying out his principle, because his interpretation and construction of the Christian consciousness was too subjective, too much separated from the objective and fixed Revelation, yet the principle itself was a sound one. Whenever a Christian creed is to be constructed, the appeal must be made to the conscious experience of the believer in Christ, as that experience has been generated and formed by the written gospel of Christ. Is the doctrine of vicarious atonement to be retained and urged in a denominational symbol? Ask him who like St. Paul is conscious that by "the deeds of the law"; that is, by an imperfect fractional obedience, which is the best that sinful man can render; "no flesh can be justified." Is the doctrine of endless punishment to be maintained and emphasized in the creed of Christendom? Ask him into whose conscience the light of inspired truth has flashed, and who vividly feels the intrinsic and eternal demerit of sin.

This method is rational, and ought not to be complained of by the belle-lettrist himself. He is prompt to affirm that only the literary and cultivated person is competent to estimate letters and culture. He contends strenuously that the theologian is not a judge of poetry and art. But upon the same principle the belle-lettrist is not qualified to decide questions in theology. In fact, he is less fitted for the function of criticism in a department that is not his own than is the theologian. For the products of genius and art address those æsthetic emotions which are natural and irrepressible in every man. Consequently, even the popular uneducated judgment of a poem or a painting contains many elements of truth, whenever the honest, unsophisticated feeling is allowed sway. But a product of profound reflection and close study of divine revelation, like a theological creed, not only addresses the abstract reasoning faculty, but demands, in order to its comprehension, a peculiar personal experience and a supernatural teaching. "The natural man receiveth not the things of the Spirit of God, for they are foolishness unto him; neither can he know them, because they are spiritually discerned." 1 Cor. 2:14.

For this reason it will be found that the theological class know much more of literature than the literary class know of theology. The literary judgments of a clergyman upon the poetry of Shakespeare and Milton would be far less liable to blundering and inaccuracy, than the theological judgments of a novelist or an artist upon the tenets of Dort and Westminster. The former might stand very respectably in a competitive examination in general literature, but the latter would certainly fail in a presbyterial examination for license to preach and teach theology.

2. In the second place, the theologian should be independent of the *sceptical literary spirit* characteristic of the present "human day."

Some forty years ago, I had occasion, in an address before a literary society, to call attention to the separation that had been brought about between literature and theology, if the nineteenth century were compared with the sixteenth and seventeenth; if the literature of the Elizabethan age were compared with that of Victoria.[1] But there is far more separation between literature and

[1] Shedd: Theological Essays, pp. 7–52.

theology now than forty years ago. The separation has become antagonism. The same process which went on in Italy at the Renaissance, has gone on during the last half-century in England and America. Literature has become humanistic, and atheistic, because it has not felt the influences of a supernatural revelation. Those refined and tasteful Greek scholars at the courts of Leo X. at Rome, and the Medici at Florence, renounced all faith in the principles of morals and religion, and the culture which they introduced into Italy, and from Italy into modern Europe, was sceptical, earthly and voluptuous. The same spirit is at work in literature, and in literary circles, at the present moment. Much has been said concerning the conflict between religion and science, but the conflict between religion and literature is far more important. The scientific class is a small one, the literary class is a large one. Where one person is made sceptical by a materializing physics, one hundred are made so by an infidel belles-lettres.

The polite literature of the last two or three decades has been greatly tinctured with disbelief, and contempt of divine revelation. Novels like those of George Eliot, and essays like those of Emerson, have preached it with a pertinacity and prolixity equal to that of the dullest of sermons. The works of Goethe, in particular, have contributed to this infidelizing and degradation of good letters. Grounded in the pantheism of Spinoza, utterly earthly and unspiritual in tone, oftentimes directly and boldly immoral, the voluminous authorship of this writer is now making itself felt in a considerable body of English and American compositions.

It is unfortunate, and in reality fraudulent, that the literature of Germany should have as its chief representative before the English-speaking races, such a mind and spirit as that of Goethe. There are worthier and greater names that have been temporarily displaced by him. The noble and lofty-minded Schiller, "whose muse was conscience," as De Staël has well said; the penetrating and discriminating Lessing, the first of critics; the graceful and imaginative Tieck; the profoundly eloquent Schelling and Schleiermacher—each and all of them have left products which an unbiassed estimate will place above anything originated by the man of Weimar. The Faust is the most sincere and earnest work of that mind so destitute of sincerity and earnestness, so marked by artistic indifference, and so devoid of the enthusiasm of genius. The heartlessness and irreverence of the mocking fiend are unquestionably drawn to the life. Mephistopheles is the only one of Goethe's numerous characters in which he actually merged his own individuality, and lost himself. Here, he becomes subjective. But what a centre-piece for the literature of a highly intellectual, highly spiritual, and highly reflective people like the Germans, is the Faust: a drama of which the whole interest turns upon the jaded sensibilities of a scholastic voluptuary, and the crimes of seduction and infanticide. Compare this low and sensual theme with the "high argument" of Milton, and the "obstinate questionings" and "blank misgivings" of a Hamlet "moving about in worlds not realized," and then wonder that the Faust could ever have been compared with the great English epic and drama.

It is this sceptical literary spirit, of which the theologian should be entirely independent. With the true literary spirit he is always in deep sympathy, because all the great products, all that is standard and perennial in every literature, is grounded in faith; in that Christianity out of which, as from a tap root, all good letters spring. But when a spurious culture, originating in a physical and luxurious civilization, proposes to remodel Divine Revelation, and teach the Christian church what its creed and worship should be, the Christian church should turn a deaf ear, and set its face as a flint. When an authorship that sneers at confession of sin and trust in redemption arrogates to itself all the intellectuality of the time, the theologian should be utterly indifferent to the claim. The demand of littérateurs that Christendom renounce the Christian faith, that the Scriptures be emptied of their meaning, that the sense of sin and the consciousness of redemption, in which the church in all time has lived, moved and had its being, be extirpated—the demand that Christianity commit suicide, should be met with a silent disdain.

I have thus, gentlemen, turned your thoughts to an important passage of Scripture, in which

St. Paul enunciates the true position of the Christian religion in reference to human science and literature. If Christianity is not a religion directly from God, the claim to superiority which he sets up for it is insolent. But if it be an infallibly inspired system, the claim is legitimate and proper. It is high time to assert the claim. Whoever really derives the religion which he teaches to his fellow creatures from the revealed word of God, should be very bold in his teaching. "Audacity, audacity, always audacity," said Danton, should be the temper of a revolutionist. It certainly should be the temper of a Christian man and a Christian herald. It was the temper of Athanasius; it was the temper of Martin Luther; it was the temper of John Calvin. These men do not seem to have been in the least troubled by the timorousness of doubt. For them, Divine Revelation was as certain as the evidence of their senses. As a consequence, they had the courage of their convictions. There is no bolder book in any language than the Institutes of Calvin. Luminous as the sky of Switzerland, and clear as the waters of lake Leman, truth is enunciated in it with a confidence which the unbeliever calls dogmatism, and the believer knows to be insight. More of this positiveness of faith and insight is needed in theoretical and practical Christianity. It is needed whenever doctrine is stated by the theologian or applied by the preacher. Creeds should be plain, explicit and firm. Preaching should be downright, direct and unhesitating.

Among the defects and faults of the seven churches of Asia, that of lukewarmness is denounced with most incisiveness by the Lord and Head of them all. " Because thou art neither cold nor hot, I will spue thee out of my mouth." Rev. 3:16. The Laodicean temper is infused into Christianity by that kind of literary influence of which we have spoken. It is the influence of dilettantism. Whenever culture becomes separated from the deep problems and truths of religion, and moves wholly in the æsthetic circles of art and fashion, it becomes shallow, pretentious, and insincere. Moral earnestness disappears from letters, and from every province affected by it. Those periods in the history of the Church, in which the theologian was converted into a littérateur, the sermon into an elegant essay, and evangelical theology into pagan ethics, were periods of lukewarmness and moral indifference. And yet they were periods of vehement opposition to evangelical religion. For when the lukewarm mind is brought into close contact with truth and there is no way of escape from it, then the moral indifference is changed into moral animosity. The mild tolerance and gentle optimism that would accept all forms of religion, now becomes an intense aversion to that particular form of religion which teaches human depravity and salvation by grace.

I have drawn one lesson from the writings of Carlyle, and will now draw another. The chief service which Carlyle did for his generation was the determined and obstinate warfare which he waged with the spirit of artistic indifference. It is one of the singular inconsistencies in his nature, that the hero whom he himself worshipped was a mere literary artist; an optimist without deep convictions or positive faith. That Thomas Carlyle should have bowed down before such an idol as Wolfgang Goethe, is one of the strangest facts in literary history. A rugged Goth, "terribly in earnest," as Jeffrey said of him, scorning and sneering at art in every form, vehement to spasm in opinions, admiring even the revolutionist and anarchist provided only he could use his tools with energy, seemingly out of all sympathy with the serene and graceful forms of the classic world —that such a mind as that should have sung the praises of one who after a brief stormy period in youth left all vehemence behind him, and for fifty years immersed himself in the placid element of Grecian culture, set beauty above truth and goodness, made art the supreme end of education, and upon principle schooled himself into profound indifference towards the religious problems of human life and destiny, is unaccountable.

In spite, however, of this man-worship, the fervid genius of the Scotchman has contributed to the restoration of positive opinions, and earnest defences of them. His repetitious denunciation of dilettantism and shams, if it be the substance of his thirty volumes, has nevertheless been a useful factor in the literary history of his generation.

What he would do for literature you, Gentlemen, should do for theology and religion. Banish from

your mind all theological dilettantism. Be in
blood earnest both theoretically and practically ;
in creed, and in preaching a creed. If at times
the flesh is weak, though the spirit is willing ; if
at times the enmity, and what is worse than enmity the lethargy of the worldly mind causes you
to shrink from delivering the unwelcome message, take refuge behind the very message itself.
Say to yourself : " It is not my doctrine, but
that of God Almighty. It is not my inspiration,
but that of my Maker and Redeemer." At the
beginning of a new year of study and preparation,
let us all remember and remind ourselves that
we are here to teach and study, not human science, or human literature, but Divine Revelation.
With this thought continually before us, let us
move forward with energy and courage.

NOTE.

Wordsworth the poet, Coleridge the poet philosopher and
critic, and Niebuhr the historian, were three minds of the
very first order in their respective provinces, and all of
them perceived the moral and intellectual inferiority of
Goethe compared with the monarchs of literature. The
following extracts evince this.

In the Memoir of Wordsworth by his nephew (Ch. lxii.),
the following estimate of Goethe is given. "Wordsworth
made some striking remarks on Goethe, in a walk on the
terrace yesterday. He thinks that the German poet is
greatly overrated, both in this country and his own. He
said, 'He does not seem to me to be a great poet in either
of the classes of poets. At the head of the first class, I
would place Homer and Shakspeare, whose universal minds
are able to reach every variety of thought and feeling with-

out bringing their own individuality before the reader. They infuse, they breathe life into every object they approach, but you never find *themselves*. At the head of the second class, those whom you can trace individually in all they write, I would place Spenser and Milton. In all that Spenser writes, you can trace the gentle affectionate spirit of the man ; in all that Milton writes, you find the exalted sustained being that he was. Now in what Goethe writes, who aims to be of the first class, you find the man himself, the artificial man, where he should not be found ; so that I consider him a very artificial writer, aiming to be universal, and yet constantly exposing his individuality, which his character was not of a kind to dignify. He had not sufficiently clear moral perceptions to make him anything but an artificial writer.' " Emerson, in his English Traits (Ch. i.), records the following judgment of Wordsworth respecting the Meister. " He proceeded to abuse Wilhelm Meister heartily. It was full of all manner of fornication. It was like the crossing of flies in the air. He had never gone further than the first part ; so disgusted was he that he threw the book across the room. I deprecated this wrath, and said what I could for the better parts of the book ; and he courteously promised to look at it again."

Coleridge, in his Table Talk, Feb. 16, 1833, speaks thus of Goethe's Faust. " The intended theme of the Faust is the consequences of a misology, or hatred and depreciation of knowledge, caused by an originally intense thirst for knowledge baffled. But a love of knowledge for itself, and for pure ends, would never produce such a misology, but only a love of it for base and unworthy purposes. There is neither originality nor progression in the Faust ; he is a ready-made conjuror from the very beginning ; the *incredulus odi* is felt from the first line. The sensuality and the thirst after knowledge are unconnected with each other. There is no whole in the poem ; the scenes are mere magic-lantern pictures, and a large part of the work is to me very flat. . . I was once pressed, many years ago, to translate the Faust ; and I so far entertained the proposal as to read the work through with great attention, and to revive in my mind my own former plan of Michael Scott. But then I considered with myself whether the time taken up in executing the translation might not more worthily be devoted to the composition of a work which, even if parallel in some points to the Faust, should be truly original in motive and execution, and therefore more interesting and valuable than any version which I could make ; and, secondly, I debated with myself whether it become my moral character to render into English, and so far, certainly, lend my countenance to language, much of which I thought vulgar, licentious, and blasphemous. I need not tell you that I never put pen to paper as a translator of Faust."

Says Niebuhr, " We are now reading Wilhelm Meister. I had never before been able to take any pleasure in this book, and was curious to see if it would be different now, as in middle age we are less one-sided than in youth, and can enjoy relative and separate beauties, even when the whole does not make an agreeable or overpowering impression on us. But it is the same as ever with me. Our language possesses, probably, nothing more elaborate and perfect in style ; it contains a multitude of acute remarks and eloquent passages ; the situations are managed with extreme ingenuity, and all the parts are in admirable keeping ; all this I can appreciate now better than formerly. But the unnaturalness of the plot, the violence with which what is beautifully sketched and executed in single groups is brought to bear upon the development and mysterious conduct of the whole, the impossibilities such a plot involves, and the thorough heartlessness which makes one linger with even the greater interest by the utterly sensual personages because they do show something akin to feeling ; the villany or meanness of the heroes, whose portraits nevertheless often amuse us—all this still makes the book revolting to me, and I get disgusted with such a menagerie of tame animals." Life and Letters, p. 232 Ed. Harper. " We are very grateful to you [Savigny] for Goethe's Life.

It no longer, indeed, reveals to us the golden and silver ages described in the first volume, but a very iron age, where even his joys and delights are a fit of intoxication which the spectator neither can nor desires to share; a strange, and to me for the most part incomprehensible kind of delirium, in which he often neglects what is most glorious. In many respects he was doubtless infected by the spirit of his age. It seems to me to be the same with Goethe as with many others who affect connoisseurship on subjects for which all true feeling is denied them. I am inclined to think that Goethe is utterly destitute of genuine susceptibility to impressions from the fine arts; that is, that he has no inward native insight which reveals to him what is really beautiful independently of the taste of the age, and still less in opposition to it; or if he ever possessed the gift as a young man at Strasburg, he lost it during the unhappy period (passed over without notice in his narrative) of his court life at Weimar, before his Italian journey, and has never recovered it. The whole tone of his mind during his travels and residence in Italy, which is most remarkable, and would alone have rendered this description of his journey more interesting than anything else you could have sent us—is it not enough to make one weep? To treat a whole nation and a whole country simply as a means of recreation for one's self; to see nothing in the wide world and nature, but the innumerable trappings and decorations of one's own miserable life; to survey all moral and intellectual greatness, all that speaks to the heart, where it still exists, with an air of patronizing superiority; or where it has been crushed and overpowered by folly and corruption, to find amusement in the comic side of the latter—is to me absolutely revolting. From these 'Travels in Italy' sprang the 'Grosscophta' and those other productions, in which all that was holy and great in his nature is shrouded from view. Cornelius is a most thorough enthusiast for Goethe, perhaps none more so; at least no man has owed so much of his inspiration to Goethe. He has a warm heart, and a fertile and profound intellect. At every spirited, lifelike description, his face lighted up with pleasure ; but as soon as that was over, resumed its expression of sadness and regret. When we closed the book for the night, and still stood talking it over, he broke silence to say, how deeply it grieved him that Goethe should have looked on Italy thus ; that either his heart must have been pulseless during that period, or else he must have stifled all emotion, so completely to keep himself aloof from the sublime, so completely to divest himself of respect for the venerable. We were all agreed that the cause of this phenomenon must perhaps be sought in an unfortunate mood, and obstinate steeling of his heart against the sense of power in the works of others, in order proudly to hold everything he saw, as it were, in his grasp ; to treat it as his property, and to depreciate it when it pleased him ; and we all lifted up our voices and lamented over the fatal court life at Weimar where Samson was shorn of his locks." Life and Letters, pp. 342–346 Ed. Harper.

COURAGE IN THE MINISTRY[1]

GENTLEMEN OF THE GRADUATING CLASS: After the animating addresses to which we have listened from your own number, you will have neither the time nor the inclination to follow very long another speaker. Let me then in a few rapid sentences say something in harmony with the hour.

You are going to work. Thus far you have been preparing for it. Now the preparation ends, and the steady, solid, heavy service begins. What you need is *courage*. This is my lesson and lecture to you on this occasion. Why should you, and why should all ministers of the gospel, be intrepid, fearless, resolute, and bold?

1. In the first place, because you serve the Son of God, the Almighty Redeemer, "by whom were all things created that are in heaven and that are in earth, visible and invisible, whether they be thrones, or dominions, or principalities, or powers." All this immense power is behind you, if you are really meek and lowly disciples and ministers of

[1] A Discourse delivered in Union Seminary.

the Lord Jesus Christ. Remember that this power is that of a living Person seated on an eternal throne. It is not the power of nature, but the power of God. It is not the energy of unconscious material laws and forces, but something infinitely mightier than they, even the intelligent and holy will of their Author and Controller. You are going forth to declare a message that has been given to you by him who holds the seven stars in his right hand, and to whom as their commissioned Mediator, the eternal Trinity have promised in solemn covenant that "His dominion shall be from sea even to sea, and from the river even to the ends of the earth." Zech. 9:10. This promise was a source of courage on a memorable occasion. When the Lord Christ was riding lowly on an ass's colt down the slopes of Olivet, when the Messenger of the covenant was on the way to his own temple (Mal. 3:1), the band of his followers brought it to mind and shouted, "Blessed is the King of Israel that cometh in the name of the Lord. Hosanna in the highest heavens." John 12:13; Matt. 21:9.

Now, constantly call to mind this Almighty power and Trinitarian promise, and be full of courage respecting the success of your errand in this world. The omnipotence of Jesus Christ needs to be remembered, in a world and an age when the power of man and of nature is greatly exaggerated and vaunted. Men who are travelling fifty miles an hour, and telegraphing a thousand miles a second, and tunnelling rivers and mountains, get the impression that they are more mighty than the generations that have gone before them; more mighty perhaps than their Maker and Redeemer. They fall into the belief that there is nothing so strong in Christianity and the gospel, as there is in arts and sciences, inventions and civilization. This temper and feeling of the century tends to hamper and discourage spiritual workers; those whose weapons are not carnal, those who have no control of armies, navies, wealth, and commerce. It is indeed true that this overestimate and exaggeration of man and of material nature, is a great misconception: for this generation is no stronger before the old standing facts of death, judgment, and eternity, than the generations that have gone before it. The whole of modern science and civilization cannot prevent death, cannot lengthen life, cannot escape eternal judgment. Before these fixed facts, one generation is as weak as another. Educated Europe is as helpless as barbaric Africa. "None of them can by any means redeem his brother, nor give to God a ransom for him, that he should still live for ever, and not see corruption." Ps. 49:7, 9. Nevertheless, in the presence of this rapid and absorbing material progress, this is forgotten, and one generation goes and another comes, full of infatuation respecting the comparative power of religion and civilization; respecting the comparative power of the Son of God and the children of men.

Be not entangled and involved in this error. Rise above the time and current, and remember continually that the Lord Jesus Christ has a direct and personal power by which he can do anything that he pleases in this sinful and lost world. All power in heaven and on earth is in his hands, in order to the progress of his gospel and the triumph of his kingdom; and he will use it when and where and how he pleases. He who called Lazarus from the grave, and will call all the dead from their graves, is mightier than nature, and is mighty to save, travelling in the greatness of his strength. And if you are meek and lowly before him; if you walk humbly by his side, and desire nothing but to make him honored and obeyed and adored here on earth; your work and message will be enforced by all of his omnipotence, and this will make you the boldest and most courageous of men.

2. In the second place, you should be of good courage, because the Almighty Son of God will personally empower you as individuals for all that he appoints you to do. "Behold, I am with you alway, even unto the end of the world. I will give you a mouth and wisdom, which all of your adversaries shall not be able to gainsay or resist." These are promises made to the Christian ministry, beginning with the Twelve Apostles, who stand at the head of the long roll. We have no doubt that these promises were made, and made good to St. John, St. Peter, and St. Paul; but so they were, and are, to every minister of Jesus Christ, past, present, and to come. These are pledges which the Lord gives to all his ministerial servants, equally and alike. It is true that we shrink from

comparing ourselves with St. John and St. Paul in respect to zeal, sincerity, and self-sacrifice in preaching the gospel. Nevertheless we belong to the same class with them. We are the successors of the Apostles in every particular, excepting those of inspiration and miraculous gifts. All that Christ promised to them as preachers of his Word and servants of his Church, he promises to us. And he promised them power: inward power to understand the truth and to teach it, and the superadded power of the Holy Ghost effectually to apply it to the hearts of men. Rely on this kind of power, and be full of courage. Do not trust to culture, science, art, either in yourselves or in society; but trust in that wonderful spiritual energy which, like the wind, bloweth where it listeth, and which, like the breath from the four winds, breathes on the slain, and they live.

This is no new lesson that I have set you, my brethren. You know these things; happy are you if you do them. When you shall have come, as some of your instructors have, very near to the close of your term of service in the Christian ministry, perhaps you will wonder as they do that there was not more of intrepidity, of courage, and of expectation, in the ministerial life. Could we but take our Lord at his word in the very opening of our ministry, could we but believe with a simple and undoubting faith his words of promise and of power, the ministry would be vastly more fruitful and vastly more blessed.

Enter then upon the ministry of reconciliation,

firmly believing that you are serving "our great God and Saviour Jesus Christ" (Titus 2:13), "by whom were all things made, and without whom was not anything made that was made." He will work in his own way, and according to the counsel of his own will. Like the stars which he made and governs, he moves without haste and without rest. Presume not to dictate the rate at which his kingdom shall make progress. Do your own piece of work to the utmost of your ability, lay it lowly at his feet, and trust him for the result and issue both of your work and of all work.

This temper will keep you calm and keep you courageous. Charles Twelfth was once hard-pressed by his powerful foe, Peter the Great. On a map of Sweden he wrote these words, "*God* has given me this kingdom, and the *devil* shall not take it away." Do the same with the map of the world. Write upon it, "God has given to his Church and ministry the whole world, and Satan shall not take it away."

With these words your instructors close their lessons and lectures to you. The connection and intercourse of three years have brought you closer and closer to them, in the bonds of Christian affection and regard. They may not have said much, but they have thought and felt much. The rapid rush of life at this centre does not permit so much of personal intercourse as is possible in more quiet retreats. But you may be very sure that we have not met you in the class-room from day to day, from month to month, from year to year, without coming to know and respect your traits of mind and heart, to perceive your fidelity, and to honor your sincere purpose to make the most of your powers and attainments, for the service of our common Lord and Master. The tie between an instructor and his scholars is high and tender. It is intellectual, grounded in the mind. And in the instance of the theological instructor and scholar, it is spiritual, grounded in the heart and a common faith. The departure of a theological class into the work of the ministry, ruptures a bond that is stronger and tenderer than that which holds a class in college to its instructors. There are common Christian beliefs, hopes, aspirations, temptations, and triumphs, that make your graduation that of younger brethren and co-laborers.

From their inmost heart, your instructors now bid you farewell and God-speed. "Wait on the Lord, be of good courage, and he shall strengthen your heart; wait, we say, on the Lord." Psa. 37:14.

INJUNCTIONS TO MINISTERS [1]

GENTLEMEN OF THE GRADUATING CLASS: The object of an address from a Seminary Faculty to a class of young men just leaving the institution for the serious work of their life must be, to speak if possible a few words that shall be "the words of the wise, which are as goads, and as nails fastened by the masters of assemblies." Eccl. 12:11. There is little time for the expansion of ideas, and no call for labored instruction. Let me, then, in the briefest manner possible, bring to your thought two or three injunctions that are suited to all times, and specially to this time.

1. In the first place, remember that your special work among mankind is, *to teach revealed truth*. You have not studied ten or fifteen years in order to conduct trade, to invent arts, to manage politics, but to convey ideas. Your function is that of instructors. And it is instruction of the highest order: that which relates to the immortality of man and the infinite part of his existence. Let nothing divert you from this kind of labor.

[1] An Address delivered in Union Seminary.

If you are asked to leave it, and take the government of a kingdom, or the control of immense material interests, say with Nehemiah, "I am doing a great work; I cannot come down." Nehem. 6:3. Devote your entire future life, be it ten years or forty, to the instruction of your fellow-men in the doctrines of the Christian religion, so that at the close of it you can say: "I have not accumulated wealth, I have not swayed senates, but I have taught the Word of God." "I have preached righteousness in the great congregation; I have not refrained my lips, O Lord, Thou knowest." Ps. 40:9.

2. In the second place, remember that he who teaches revealed truth to mankind, *glorifies God in the highest degree possible to a feeble instrument like man.* He who erects a temple for divine worship honors God. He who founds a university or builds a hospital from Christian love for man, honors God. He who performs any kind of Christian service, be it a gift of cold water, honors God. All such service is accepted and rewarded. But the very highest service which any human creature can render here upon earth to the Triune God, is to preach his Word. When Christ chose twelve men to be the teachers of mankind in the truths of his religion, he exalted them above all the Cæsars. What emperor, what poet, what philosopher, to-day, stands so high in the scale as St. Paul? When Christ calls a man to the ministry of the Word, he calls him to do a work for which he is himself personally more concerned than he is for any other.

The secret of the interest which God takes in the truths which you are to teach, lies in the fact that they centre in the redeeming work of the Son of God. Redemption is a Trinitarian transaction. God the Father, Son, and Holy Ghost originate and execute it. Hence their infinite concern for its success. We forget, in our puzzle over the problem of sin, that the dreadful effects of sin are not confined to man the sinner. The permission of evil has not only ruined man, but has involved the merciful Godhead in an immense self-sacrifice. The entrance of sin into this lower world, *has cost God the holy more than it has cost man the sinner*. Not all men together have suffered so much, or will suffer so much, for their own sin, as God incarnate has vicariously suffered for it. The Lord Jesus Christ can say to every sinner upon earth : " You have not resisted unto blood, striving against sin. You have not in anguish cried, If it be possible, let this cup pass from me. You have not in agony exclaimed, My God, my God, why hast thou forsaken me ? "

This stupendous self-sacrifice on the part of one of the Trinitarian persons, accounts for the Divine zeal for that system of truth connected with the crucifixion of the Lord of glory, and explains God's interest in the preaching of the gospel. God infinitely desires the success of it ; and the success of it he has made to depend upon the teaching of it to all the world by the Christian ministry. Whoever, therefore, preaches Christ the Lamb of God that taketh away the sin of the world, does a human act, than which there is none higher in the Divine estimation. In the great day, there will be many rewards of varying value for varying services. Our Lord will speak an applauding word to every faithful disciple. But to that minister of the Word who, utterly unknown to the busy secular world, lived and died among the benighted heathen, he will address a plaudit to which the mass of the church is not entitled: "Well done; for thou hast preached my cross and passion; thou hast, instrumentally, sprinkled my blood upon human souls." "I saw," says St. John, "the souls of them that were beheaded for the witness of Jesus, and for the Word of God; and they lived and reigned with Christ a thousand years. But the rest of the dead lived and reigned not, until the thousand years were finished." Rev. 20:4, 5.

3. In the third place, remember that he honors God most highly, who *preaches God's truth most truly*. When Dante reaches the ninth and last heaven of Paradise, he hears from Beatrice a vehement denunciation of certain theologians and preachers of those days, whose ignorance or avarice induced them to substitute their own inventions for the pure word of the Gospel. She then tells him that:

> "Christ said not to his first conventicle,
> 'Go forth and preach impostures to the world.'
> But gave them truth to build on; and the sound
> Was mighty on their lips: nor needed they,

> Beside the gospel, other spear or shield,
> To aid them in their warfare for the faith."
>
> *Paradise*, xxix., 115-19.

All truth is powerful in proportion as it is thoroughly stated. A half-truth is weaker than a whole-truth. Dilutions are not pungent. The secret of intellectual power is intellectual intensity. When there is a zeal for God's house, the zeal eats up both the speaker and hearer. This was that devouring energy that made the Son of God so earnest, when, on the way to Jerusalem and the bitter cross, he strode on before the disciples and "they were amazed." Mark 10:32. The Redeemer never stated truth languidly or hesitatingly. His double, "Verily, verily, I say unto you," implies that his perception was thorough, and his belief undoubting.

Now, this must be the style of his ministers. They are ambassadors in his place, and they must not appear before men querying and doubting, but asserting and demonstrating. They cannot, indeed, speak with that almighty and overwhelming power that belonged to their Divine Lord; and he does not require this of them. The Lord Jesus Christ was never foiled in an argument; and he always silenced his opponent. He spake as never man spake. But the minister of Christ can possess some of his Master's power. If he follows him closely, if he studies him closely, if he communes with him closely, he will derive from him some of that spiritual energy, that sincere downrightness, and that holy boldness, which compels the attention and respect of the human mind.

Endeavor, then, during the twenty or forty years that you shall be giving religious instruction to your fellow-men, endeavor to present the *whole* truth. Adopt no hesitating and half-way views. Make no hesitating and half-hearted statements. Preach the truth *truly*.

4. In the fourth place, remember that *revealed truth must be preached exclusively*. When the Emperor Galerius lay dying, in the hope that the God of the Christians might possibly give him the help which all his supplication to the heathen divinities had not succeeded in obtaining, he issued an edict abolishing the persecuting laws against the Christians, permitting them to erect their sacred edifices, and to perform their public worship unmolested. But with this condition: that they should do nothing to weaken the old religion of the Roman Empire, and should not attempt to convert any one from the religion of his ancestors to the new Christianity. (Mosheim's Commentaries, ii., 452.) The requirement was, that Christianity should be only one of several religions: *e pluribus unum*. The Christians could not accept such a deliverance from persecution as this. They had received a commission to preach the gospel to every creature under heaven, and to proclaim to the wide world, with all its nationalities and religions, that there is no other name, under heaven, given among men, whereby they must be saved, but the name of Jesus Christ, the Son of God.

They understood Christianity to be an exclusive religion. They were not willing to place the bust of Jesus Christ in the Pagan pantheon with those of Jupiter and Apollo. They would go to the stake, rather than promise not to endeavor to convert men from paganism to Christianity.

Now, this must be the spirit of Christ's ministers in all time. They cannot consent to put the Christian gospel among the *religiones licitæ*, the allowable religions. This is the demand now made upon the Christian church, in some quarters. A class of popular but superficial writers are actually proposing to Christendom that it receive religious instruction from Boodha, and get divine illumination from the " Light of Asia." Naturalism, both in literature and science, denies the exclusiveness of Christ's gospel, and with Pope, in his Universal Prayer, calls upon the

> Father of all, in every age,
> In every clime adored,
> By saint, by savage, and by sage,
> Jehovah, Jove, or Lord.

To grant this demand, is to destroy Christianity. Because it proceeds upon the assumption that man has no sin that requires atonement and remission, and no corruption that necessitates regeneration. This theory of one universal religion made up of a conglomeration of all religions, supposes the essential soundness of human nature, and denies the doctrines of man's guilt and Christ's vicarious sacrifice. It implies that humanity, by means of its natural religious sentiment and its progressive tendencies, can lift itself up from lower to higher grades of character and condition.[1]

Now if there is any one postulate more antagonistic than another to the claims of Christ and his religion, it is this. And if there is any one demand made by this portion of the educated classes that is to be more determinedly repelled than another, it is this. "Think not," said the Founder of Christianity, "that I am come to send peace on earth: I came not to send peace, but a sword." Matt. 10:34. Let no man think that those cardinal doctrines and facts of the Christian religion which are grounded in the assumption of the fall and ruin of all mankind, can be made to harmonize with any schemes that deny or overlook this. Christianity will recognize whatever elements of ethical truth there are in the natural ethnic religions, expelling the large amount of error mixed with them, but will never stoop to be classified with them, or to be put upon an equality with them.

But some man will say: "This will make the Christian minister haughty and intolerant. This will bring back the middle ages, and the tyranny of the Papal church." Not so, if the Christian minister counts himself as the mere servant, and an unworthy servant, of his divine Lord and

---

[1] The proposed Congress of All Religions at the Columbian Exposition looks in this direction, and tends in its practical influence to equalize the ethnic religions with Christianity.

Master. If he regards himself as teaching the results of his own investigation, and the product of his own discoveries in religion, then, indeed, to proclaim an exclusive religion will be the height of vanity, and also of absurdity. But if he sinks and buries out of sight his own feeble and fallible personality, in the wisdom and authority of divine revelation, and of the high command: "Go, preach my gospel to every creature," he will not be a proud man, but a very lowly one. When Moses and Aaron, in a moment of egotism, said to the people: "Hear now, ye rebels; must we fetch you water out of this rock?" (Numbers 20:10), their pride wakened the divine displeasure, and they were chastised by not being permitted to bring the people into the promised land. But when Moses said to Jehovah: "If thy presence go not with me, carry us not up hence" (Ex. 33:15), he was the meekest of men.

Neither need the minister of the Christian religion be feared on the ground of intolerance. The days of bloody persecution are over. The conflict now is that of ideas and opinions. Every creed is tolerated. The atheist can blaspheme his Creator to his heart's content on a public platform, with none to molest him or make him afraid. A polygamous community dwells unharmed in the midst of Christian institutions. He who wants more toleration than this, wants, in the phrase of Sancho, "better bread than can be made of wheat." But some men do ask for more. They require that opinions upon the grave and solemn subjects of human responsibility and destiny which clash with their own, be surrendered. They call it intolerance, when a Christian denomination holds a strong creed, and insists that its clergy hold it, and preach it. They denominate it bigotry, when Christian churches refuse to accept certain tenets, or to do anything that will promote their extension among men. Now if this is intolerance, it must be tolerated. Opinions must be left free. Every man must be permitted to think for himself, and form positive and fixed views if he please. And so must every *association* of men. It is too late for the "liberal" theologian to say to an ecclesiastical denomination, "You shall not be Calvinists, nor require that those who voluntarily join you shall be so likewise or be expelled from the body."

When, therefore, great and influential masses of men organize themselves into churches founded upon creeds derived in their opinion from an infallible revelation, they are not to be charged with an intolerant and persecuting spirit. The conflict between them and their opponents is largely intellectual, though not wholly so, because the heart is concerned as well as the head. It is a question of logic as well as faith. The closest reasoner, not the inquisitor with thumb-screw and rack, will carry the day. If Celsus argues more powerfully than Origen, Hume than Butler, Strauss than Neander; if in the long sweep of the ages skepticism evinces a purer reason and a deeper intuition than faith, then skepticism will conquer the human intellect, and take it captive. Let both grow together, then, until the harvest, and as the Christian church brings no charge of bigotry and intolerance against the disbeliever, so neither let the disbeliever bring this charge against the Christian church.

GENTLEMEN OF THE GRADUATING CLASS: You stand now on the threshold of ministerial life. The years of preparation and public irresponsibility are behind you. Before you, are those of leadership and accountability. You are now to guide opinions, and particularly the religious opinions of men. Upon the clergy, depends very greatly the mode of thinking, and the tone of feeling, in the Christian church. If you are clear, bold, and firm, in your statement of divine truth, you can be tracked by the positive and energetic churches which will respect you, and cling to you with hooks of steel; and you will be remembered long after this brief life is over, by the transmitted vigor and force of your ministry. St. Paul exhorted Timothy to "make full proof" of his ministry. This meant a concentration of his power; a full performance of the duties of his calling. Those of us who can look back over forty years of intellectual and spiritual service can see a failure in this respect. If called to pass over it once more, they would endeavor to live a more simple, a more sincere, a more undivided life. The glory of God, the honor of Christ the Lord, is the one motive that simplifies and concentrates human service. There is no scattering of energy, when that end is before a man. We are not our own. We did not create ourselves; we do not uphold ourselves; and we do not redeem ourselves. But we live and labor too much as if we had a private and independent existence of our own. We do not lose ourselves in God, and hence our work is mixed with subtle references to self. This makes us anxious; and anxiety weakens and discourages. Endeavor to discharge your coming ministry in simplicity and godly sincerity. Then you will not be cast down by seeming failure, or elated by success. Your ministerial life will be calm; the close it will be eternal peace; and the result of it a far greater amount of usefulness than can be reached by any other method.

"The Lord bless you, and keep you. The Lord make his face to shine upon you, and be gracious unto you. The Lord lift up his countenance upon you, and give you peace." This ancient benediction your instructors utter with all their heart, as they now bid you a most hopeful, and a most affectionate, Farewell.

ONE TRUTH FOR ALL PULPITS

"THERE are diversities of operations, but it is the same God which worketh all in all," said St. Paul to the Corinthian church, and to the church universal. By this he teaches, among other things, that all Christian ministers ought to hold the same fundamental truth, though they may preach it in different modes and manners. The same Holy Ghost employs the same doctrines of law and gospel, exerts the same divine influence, and produces the same personal experience, when he makes a Christian of John Calvin as when he makes a Christian of John Wesley. But the treasure is in an earthen vessel, and there is a difference in the way in which it comes out of the vessel. Two equally good men may not be equally successful in describing their own religious experience to others. But the description of the religious experience is substantially a statement of religious doctrine. If the one man is able to state it with great fulness and self-consistence while the other reports it with less fulness and logical consistency, it is plain that to a mere student of theological systems the two men will so differ as perhaps to lead to the conclusion that they do not believe the same fundamental truth, and do not have a common religious experience. But this is an error. He who searches the heart perceives that the two men agree in their view of their own sinfulness and of Christ's redemption. They hold the same gospel truth, and therefore they are brethren in the Lord. Their religious experience, which is what God has wrought in them, is the same evangelical experience that belongs to all members of the one invisible church of Christ.

This diversity in the expression and statement of evangelical truth appears also in the preacher as much as in the theologian. And it is increased in this instance by the operation of other causes. There is more play of the imagination, more illustration, more presentation of truth in loose and flowing costume, in the instance of the orator than in that of the school-divine. It is not strange that statements of doctrine before an auditory should be less guarded and less precise than before a theological class. Some one has defined eloquence to be exaggeration. He was probably like the philosopher Kant an enemy to anything but the close and exact propositions of logic, and put his dislike to rhetoric in this peculiar definition. Yet there is truth in it. Discourse for the people must have a dash and rush that are out of place in the closet of the thinker. St. Paul alludes to this when he speaks of himself as "planting," and of Apollos as "watering." Logic plants, and rhetoric waters.

The great apostle to the Gentiles tacitly conceded an eloquence of speech to Apollos which God had denied to himself. His own function was to write the epistle to the Romans, while his coadjutor was to be "an eloquent man mighty in the Scriptures." We do not of course deny eloquence to St. Paul; the speech on Mars' Hill is powerful Demosthenean eloquence. But, comparatively, he was more of a logician than a rhetorician. It was the converse with Apollos. But with this "diversity of operation" there was the same spirit. The same God the Holy Ghost wrought the same faith, the same hope, the same religious experience, in both of these men.

We come, then, to the conclusion for which we have made these preliminary statements, namely, that in all Christian pulpits, however different may be the mental and oratorical characteristics of the preachers, the same kind of religious *impression* ought to be made and the same fundamental *truth* ought to be taught. The result of logical preaching, of imaginative preaching, of illustrative preaching, ought, with the divine blessing, to be the same. And what is this result? Plainly the conviction of men, if they ought to be convicted; their conversion, if they need to be converted; their sanctification, if they require it.

Here, then, we have a test by which to try the preachers of the day, and of all time. If a pulpit orator artfully avoids all those parts of divine revelation which treat of sin and perdition, and never preaches a sermon that awakens fears that the soul may be lost forever, it will not do to say that he has the same spirit with St. Paul, only there is a "diversity of operation." There is one impression which St. Paul made, which he never makes. This is something more than a rhetorical difference between him and the inspired apostle. There is a difference in doctrinal belief.

The defect, and the fatal defect, in some of the popular preaching of this age, is that under the covert of mere rhetoric without logic, of mere illustration without argument, of mere story-telling without religious point or pertinence, of mere figures and tropes, men are persuaded to believe that religion is a very lovely song, and that all men are naturally religious because they enjoy the music. The impression made, and it is the impression that decides the character and value of the preaching—the impression actually made upon the audience is this: "Get rid of your religious fears and you are all right. If the ostrich will only stick his head into the sand, he is perfectly safe."

DOCTRINAL PREACHING

An ignorant but well-meaning member of a Christian church was once asked how a certain minister had impressed the congregation by his preaching. The congregation were more than usually susceptible to religious impressions. A revival was in progress. The good man had this fact in his mind, in his answer to the inquiry. "He did not do well at all," was the reply, "he came down and preached a *doctrine* sermon right in the midst of the interest!" We fear that this notion that doctrinal preaching is ill-adapted to promote the best interests of a church, is more common than it ought to be among those who are commanded to account those elders "worthy of double honor who labor in the word and doctrine," and who are bidden to see that the "name of God and his doctrine be not blasphemed."

The prejudice against doctrinal preaching arises from two causes. The first is the aversion of the heart to God's revealed truth. Whenever this truth is stated doctrinally, it is stated clearly and pointedly; and the point pierces. It is hard to kick against the pricks. Men do not object to have the truth respecting sin, death, and hell presented poetically and sentimentally, because in this form it gives no trouble; but when it is stated plainly and accurately, they wince. Men are never convicted by a poem; they are by a doctrine.

The second objection to doctrinal preaching springs from the natural indolence of the human mind. It costs more mental effort to listen to a well-reasoned sermon, than to a flowery one that starts from no premises and comes to no conclusion. We do not believe that it is a complete definition of sin to say that it is laziness, but it is safe theology to say that every sinner is lazy. When, therefore, clear and logical statements of Christian truth are made, they require an effort on the part of the hearer to follow them from beginning to end. This effort he is unwilling to make, and instead of repenting of his sin and forsaking it, he decries doctrinal preaching.

But the fault is not always in the hearer. The preacher is often at fault. The clergy are affected by their congregations. Finding a disinclination in the congregation to listen to cogent preaching, to "reasoning out of the Scriptures," the minister yields, and shrinks from the plain and solemn message which God has bidden him to deliver, and which he promised to deliver when he took his ordination vow. There are many reasons against such a course which we cannot mention in this brief article. Passing over all those grave and conclusive reasons which relate to the glory of Christ and the salvation of souls, we call attention to the fact that the neglect of doctrinal preaching results in the decline and decay of the preacher's powers. A man who never studies and preaches doctrine grows weaker day by day. We do not now allude to spiritual power. Of course he becomes less serious and holy, and more and more worldly. But we speak of intellectual power. A doctrine is a clear and accurate statement. The doctrine of the atonement, for example, is such an account of the sufferings and death of Jesus Christ as causes a hearer or reader to understand distinctly why Jesus Christ suffered and died, and for whom. Now, it is an inevitable effect of making sharp and strong statements to make the mind sharp and strong. We observe this in the legal profession, from which the clerical profession in these days of loose and vague declamation ought to learn some things. That lawyer who is noted for the power of stating a case, is noted for his mental acumen and ability. But the lawyer's case is the lawyer's "doctrine." It is a plain and accurate statement of a fact or facts. He has been employed to make it, and the more precise and exact the style in which he does this, the better is his client pleased, and the more likely is he to get the verdict.

Some preachers take a very different course from that of the lawyer. What would be thought of a lawyer who should decry Blackstone's Commentaries and Coke upon Lyttleton, upon the ground that they are too doctrinal, and that juries are not interested in reasoning and logic, and should prepare for the court-room by the perusal of the trial of Mr. Pickwick, and attempt to obtain legal knowledge from Serjeant Buzfuz? And yet certain preachers who contrive to attract large miscellaneous audiences pursue a similar course. They not only neglect doctrinal theology, but they vilify it. They do not deduce from the Scriptures a system of infallible truth, which they convey to the understandings of their hearers, but they expatiate and oftentimes vociferate upon some moral or immoral subject to which they attach a Biblical text—a short tail to their long kite.

BONED PREACHING

The value of truth is never more evident than in a period of revival in the churches. When the Holy Spirit is poured out, and operates as a Spirit of conviction, if he finds the doctrines of revelation already laid up in the mind, he employs them in bringing men to a sense of their sin and spiritual need. Consequently those communities who have been the best instructed by a faithful ministry of the Word, are those who derive most benefit from a religious awakening. It is to be hoped that the present gracious visitation of the churches throughout the country, by the Divine Spirit, will result, among other things, in a deeper sense of the importance of sound doctrine. And it is matter of thankfulness that the large masses which during the past weeks have been listening to the preacher and singer at the Hippodrome, have been taught the vital truths of revelation. Not the least of the good effects of the labors of Moody and Sankey is the restoration of the doctrines of sin and grace, of guilt and atonement, to their proper place in the popular mind.

For some years past it has been a discouraging characteristic, that large audiences have been drawn together and held by a style of preaching that disparaged and oftentimes ridiculed evangelical truth. A great congregation and a popular speaker have, too frequently, been equivalent to reckless teaching and reckless hearing. The masses have been told that theology is a skeleton, and should be buried out of sight with other skeletons. Distinct and definite statements, especially those that relate to man's guilt and danger, to the wrath of God and the necessity of fleeing from it, have been stigmatized as dry bones. That incorrigible jester, Sydney Smith, told an old lady who asked him how he managed to keep cool during the very hot weather, that he took off his flesh and sat in his bones. These preachers reverse this method. They take out their bones and sit in their flesh. And what a mess they make of theology. What a flabby pulp is their sermonizing. Their discourse has no organization. "A very eloquent talker indeed," said Hazlitt of a certain person, "if you let him start with no premises and come to no conclusion." The remark was untrue of the distinguished man respecting whom the acrid Hazlitt said it, but it is strictly true of certain pulpiteers who during the last decade have been styled by the newspapers the greatest preachers of the age. Some of these sermons have been published, and constitute several volumes. He who should sit down and endeavor to deduce from them a series of truths for the guidance of man in his search for salvation, would be greatly perplexed. Orthodoxy upon one page is contradicted by heresy on the next. The reader is told in one breath that he must seek salvation, and in the next that he is already safe enough. Regeneration is now the work of God, and now man's self-improvement. From the mass of self-contradictions, however, the hearer is certain to derive the impression that the looser statement is the better of the two. The orthodoxy is, after all, merely a tub thrown for the whale to play with, while the harpoon is being aimed at his vitals. In this way the popular audience has been wheedled into the belief and reception of deadly error, under the guise of evangelical religion, and from a preacher of evangelical connections. From the pulpit and through the press, this kind of religious teaching has spread through society, and has seriously weakened the religious faith of the masses.

There are indications, now, of a change for the better. We hope that the worst has been seen, and that the tide has turned. The so-called "liberal" religion begins to be looked at suspiciously. Men fear that loose theory is likely to end in loose practice, lax theology in lax morality. The common sense of men cannot be abused too long. The popular audience, after a time, becomes weary of self-contradictions, and desires to be fed, as St. Paul fed his audiences, "with knowledge and understanding." May we not expect that as the masses are now ready to go, day after day of the secular week, to hear the plain and unadorned, but thoroughly earnest and pungent statement of evangelical truth, from men who believe what they say, so they will continue to like this style, and that the period of *boned preaching* for the masses is over and gone.

THE EVILS OF PULPIT NOTORIETY

A SECULAR journal moralizes over the confession of a prominent witness in a certain trial, that in his younger days he worshipped great men, but that since he had come to know them better, he was "sick" of them. The journalist seems in his moralizing to make no distinction between the varieties of great men, but puts them all into one catalogue; as Macbeth says that "hounds and greyhounds, mongrels, spaniels, curs, shoughs, water-rugs, and demi-wolves, are cleped all by the name of dogs." He mentions Alexander, Cæsar, Washington, and Hamilton in connection with the particular "great man" by whom this witness in his youthful and immature years had been dazzled, as if such a juxtaposition were not ridiculous.

And yet this journalist is only repeating the vulgar error of confounding notoriety with fame. Because an individual happens to be the town-talk, unthinking persons suppose that he thereby goes into history, and becomes the theme of admiration for a nation, or for mankind. Nothing is easier than to get notoriety, and nothing is more difficult than to acquire fame. The arts that promote the former defeat the latter. He who would gain a lasting reputation, in any department of human effort, must cultivate his powers so highly and exert them so conscientiously, as to preclude the indiscriminating and noisy applause of a narrow circle of relatives, friends, and dependents. Notoriety always supposes more or less of personal acquaintance and relationship; fame supposes none at all. A noted politician, or a noted actor, or a noted preacher, derives his reputation from the crowd that gathers about him when he makes a public appearance, and the celebrity which he enjoys is due to individual traits and peculiarities, more than to those solid excellences that remain the same for all time and under all circumstances.

It is here that the evil influence of mere pulpit notoriety upon the church and society is apparent. The declamatory and sensational preacher gathers around him only a particular class. It is a class marked by defects that require to be removed rather than strengthened. They are commonly the very same defects which the preacher has himself. Like priest, like people. He abhors doctrine, and they abhor it. He talks metaphors, relates anecdotes, and raises laughter, and they like metaphors, anecdotes, and laughter. He favors loose and easy-going ethics, and they enjoy the same. In this way, the preacher speedily becomes the "great man" of his congregation, and then

> "Like Cato gives his little senate laws,
> And sits attentive to his own applause."

The injurious effect of notoriety upon the individual himself who is so unfortunate as to have it is manifold. It is almost fatal to personal piety. The devout and saintly men in the history of the Church, have not been local celebrities. No deep and pure character is formed under the intoxicating stimulus of a crowd of partisans. On the contrary, infirm virtue, sad lapses, and great scandals are apt to come in connection with such influences. The effect upon the preacher in puffing him up with self-conceit is remarkable. It is very difficult for him to think others better than himself, and to condescend to men of low estate. Bolingbroke tells the story of a popular member of a French parliament who being overcome by his own eloquence was overheard after his speech muttering devoutly to himself, "Lord, now lettest thou thy servant depart in peace, for mine eyes have seen thy salvation." This extravagance in secular oratory can be matched in the records of ecclesiastical. Some preachers have had as absurd notions of their own superiority as this French deputy had, and some congregations have been as crazy about their idol.

It is a dark day for a church, and it betokens great spiritual decline when the people cease to be content with thoughtful, devout, and scriptural teaching, and clamor for celebrated preachers. The demand will create the supply, and the church will be filled with declaimers and ecclesiastical charlatans. There will be no truly great men produced; and what is far worse no truly good men.

There will be abundance of notoriety, but no fame; and what is worse no piety. In thus foolishly and wickedly trying to find their life, both the preachers and the people will have lost it.

OVERESTIMATED POPULARITY

A VERY common way of defending heresy or error is to direct attention to its popularity. One preacher who departs from the evangelical faith is drawing a crowd, while another who proclaims the old and simple faith of the gospel has only an ordinary audience, or perhaps a thin one. When the former is arraigned before the proper authorities, and is asked why he has violated his ordination vows, with many persons it is thought to be a conclusive answer to say that his church is crowded, and that the pews are all rented. The small audience of the orthodox minister is pointed at as proof that orthodoxy is antiquated and useless, and that the new doctrine is what the times demand. Public notoriety is thus made the criterion of Christianity.

There are several fallacies in this popular judgment. One is in making notoriety the equivalent of reputation or fame. Macaulay says that Wordsworth worked on in his own chosen line of poetic thought careless of contemporary opinion, "conscious that he was unpopular, but certain that he would be immortal." There were many local and temporary poetic reputations in Wordsworth's day that obscured his for the time being ; but this generation has forgotten those celebrities, while the name of Wordsworth is one of the permanent influences of England.

But another fallacy relates to the fact of the popularity itself. Error is not so popular as is supposed or claimed. Take an example. The late Theodore Parker is said to have had an audience of two thousand persons, and this was often cited in proof of the immense popularity of infidelity in the city of Boston. But Parker was the only preacher of the sort, and preached only half a day. The edifice where he spoke was within easy reach of a million of people. Did it evince any very wonderful popularity of the preaching of Theodore Parker, that some two thousand persons out of a million were sufficiently interested to go and hear him? Put Parkerism to the same test that the gospel is put to, and see how it would fare. Suppose that there had been ten or twenty orators preaching "theism" within the radius of five miles, would there have been ten or twenty audiences each of two thousand persons? Parker had no brethren in the ministry. He was the only one of the species. He had all the hearers who wanted to hear this kind of doctrine. If he had been compelled to share his audience with a half-dozen others, he would have had a smaller following than the dullest and dryest of orthodox ministers. The popularity of a tenet is to be measured by its reception by the great mass of the people; by the number of those who proclaim it, and by the number of the audiences that rally to hear it. Because one man with one dancing bear gathers quite a crowd in the street, it does not follow that dancing bears are popular with the whole community. Multiply the bears, and they would immediately become unpopular. Increase the number of heretical or infidel preachers, and their audience rooms would be deserted. There is not enough of vigor and vitality in error to bear repetition like orthodoxy from a thousand pulpits and a thousand preachers. As it is, the errorist has no immediate successor. Theodore Parker's congregation is scattered. Infidelity has no power of permanent growth or continuity.

The same remark is true of those preachers who, though not sceptics like Parker, are lax and erroneous in their teachings. Their popularity also is overrated. The number in this class is small, compared with that large body of evangelical preachers and pastors who are expounding the Scriptures and proclaiming the one old doctrine of Paul and Peter. The number of persons who wish to hear them, is small compared with the whole body of devout and intelligent persons who make up the various evangelical denominations. A pulpit celebrity, with just enough of Biblical doctrine to clear him from the charge of infidelity, and more than enough of human error to make his preaching piquant and taking with a certain class, establishes himself in some metropolitan centre.

He is alone, and has for his audience all of this "ilk" that can get around his pulpit. It is a large audience compared with each of the hundred audiences that are listening to gospel sermons within the same circumference of five or ten miles, and the hasty inference is drawn that this man and his doctrine is more popular than St. Paul would be, preaching such dogmas as are contained in the ninth chapter of his epistle to the Romans. But multiply this celebrity by ten, and see what the size of his audience would be.

This overestimate of the popularity of error may be illustrated again by the theatre. There is considerable similarity between a sensational preacher and a celebrated actor. It will generally be found that the talent of the former is largely histrionic. It is often remarked of such a one that he would make a good actor. Take away from him his power of mimicry and kindred gifts, and he would be shorn of much of his popular talent. Now, as one sees a theatre pouring out its crowd at the close of the performance, he might infer that the great mass of the community are play-goers. But the fact is, that only a small minority of the entire population of even such a worldly city as New York habitually attend the theatre. While hundreds are listening to the actor, thousands are in the quiet and privacy of their homes. Ten or fifteen theatres suffice for a million of people.

When, therefore, it is said in defence of lax and unevangelical preachers and preaching, that they draw a large audience, let the question be asked: *How many* large audiences do they draw? Of how many audiences, large or small, does this lax and unevangelical *denomination* consist? Is it popular enough to be a denomination at all? Or do its preachers and audiences live as parasites upon the evangelical denominations?

WIT AND HUMOR IN PREACHING

The maxim that "ridicule is the test of truth" is attributed to the Earl of Shaftesbury. These particular words are not to be found in his writings, but a sentiment resembling them can be. It is the maxim of the sceptic. Voltaire proceeded upon it, when he subjected the doctrines of Christianity to a wit that has never been excelled for point and brilliancy. The infidel, generally, whatever be the grade of his knowledge and culture, betakes himself to ridicule as an easy and ready method of attacking sacred things. What little influence Thomas Paine has exerted, is due to his coarse and racy derision; and Theodore Parker will be remembered chiefly for his vigorous scoffing at truths which for ages have been enshrined in the reverence and affection of Christendom. But the maxim has never been accepted as correct. If an opponent has nothing but ridicule to offer against a system, he will fail in overthrowing it, because the human intellect demands reasons and reasoning as the ground of its decisions. The wages of a joke is a laugh, and of a great joke a horse-laugh; but the human understanding craves arguments. Men may enjoy the keenness and ingenuity of the witticism, but will not allow their opinions to be determined by it, unless they are shallow-pates and triflers themselves; for it is immediately perceived that there is nothing that cannot be ridiculed. Even the august and awful being of God may be converted into a subject of derision, provided there be no reverence in man to deter him from blasphemy. Even the sad experiences of human life; sickness, suffering, and death itself; may have a ridiculous aspect put upon them, provided there be no decency and no shame to prevent.

Conceding, then, the falsity of the maxim in this form of statement, how stands the case with its converse? May we say that "ridicule is the test of error?" Error, unquestionably, has a side that is intrinsically contemptible. This is one of the points of difference between right and wrong, truth and falsehood. There is nothing really and truly despicable, and so worthy of scorn and derision, in either the good, the true, or the beautiful. But in their contraries there is nothing that is not deserving of ridicule and contempt. Hence, to subject error to wit is to subject it to a legitimate test. This is by no means the only test. The chief dependence in this instance, also, must be placed upon logic. Error must be reasoned out of existence. Men demand arguments when they are asked to give up opinions which are dear to their self-love and corruption of heart.

Still, after the strong and cogent reasons have been presented, it is right and proper to pour in upon the exploded falsehood the flame of sarcasm, and burn it up as under a compound blow-pipe. The Scriptures themselves, though sparing in their use of this quality, do nevertheless employ it. There is no moral scorn more contemptuous and withering than that which fills the ridicule which Elijah, under the divine afflatus, poured upon the priests of Baal, unless it be that which Isaiah expends upon the manufacturers of idols.

But the maxim that "ridicule is the test of error" needs to be cautiously used; and it is to press this point that all our previous remarks have been made. Wit is good only in connection with logic. Alone, and by itself, it is like faith without works. For all purposes of conviction, "it is dead, being alone." When, therefore, the writer or speaker neglects instruction and argumentation, and overflows with light and laughable matter, he will accomplish little in actually confirming the good principles, or eradicating the evil principles of his readers or hearers. Leviathan is not so tamed. Here is the defect in much of the attack which the newspaper nowadays makes upon crime. We have been struck and saddened by the tenor of this species of writing. The crime, instead of being discussed and condemned with seriousness and earnestness as offence against both human and divine law, and against the best interests of society, is merely held up to ridicule. It is not defended, of course; but the impression that is made is that the criminal was a simpleton, a fellow without brain enough to keep himself out of trouble. If any one will look over the files and read what has been published in the journals of this city respecting the late notorious assassination, he will understand our meaning. There is a strange and mournful absence of high-minded reasoning and solemn denunciation.

The pulpit is not altogether free from the same charge. A certain class of preachers rely more upon wit and ridicule than upon reason and argument. Their audiences expect to be amused, and should they be disappointed in their expectations for any considerable length of time, would fall off. Hence, preachers of this order work the vein of mirth and ridicule. It is a dangerous trade; as dangerous as that of Shakspeare's gatherer of samphire. For no just, true, and complete view of truth is given by this method; and even the view given of error is oftentimes unfair, and always inadequate and feeble. Men cannot be laughed or ridiculed out of sin, if for no other reason than that laughter is only a movement of the diaphragm. Bodily exercise profiteth little.

THE CREDULITY OF INFIDELITY

It is a remark of Pascal, one of the most subtle and discriminating minds, that nothing is more credulous than infidelity. This seems to be a paradox, but its truth is frequently proved by actual examples. One has recently come to our notice in the case of Robert Dale Owen. This, in some respects, well-meaning man was a disbeliever in divine revelation, and yet became the dupe of an impudent and unblushing pretender to supernatural power. He did not think the miracles of the Bible to be supported by sufficient evidence, yet placed credit in the impostures of the Holmes mediums. That he might not miss any of the revelations, he went to Philadelphia to reside, and pinned his faith in a future immortality not upon the words of Jesus Christ but of Katie King. When this woman confessed that she had conspired with others to impose upon him and others like-minded with him, and that she was no spirit, but a woman with flesh and bones like other mortals, Owen was so overcome with the disclosure that his reason reeled and he became insane.

Looking at the facts in this case, it is easy to

see that the sceptic is more credulous than the Christian. Owen believed what the great majority disbelieved. This is one mark of credulity. The little coterie in Philadelphia who trusted Katie King's assertions, were a handful compared with the great multitude of Philadelphians who put no faith in her revelations. The masses of Philadelphia believed the Biblical miracles and rejected those of the spiritualist. Owen made his choice between the supernaturalism of infidelity and that of Christianity, and in accepting the former went with the credulous minority rather than with the believing majority. When our Lord wrought miracles in Jerusalem he carried the majority with him. The believers, in this instance, were not a handful, but the whole city in a mass. Only a small party, the Pharisees and the rulers who hated him and his doctrine, endeavored to stem the tide that was coming in by suggesting that he cast out devils by Beelzebub the prince of the devils. Even they did not dispute the fact of the miracle. In reference to the greatest of the miracles, the resurrection of Lazarus, the Pharisees were compelled to give up the contest in despair, saying, " Perceive ye how ye prevail nothing? behold the world is gone after him."

Again, in making such a choice, Owen selected that species of supernaturalism which had been tried at best only a few weeks, and rejected that species which had been tried for nineteen centuries. Katie King had been seen in the twilight and in the dark by a small number. The Christian revelation had been the study in broad day of a multitude whom no man can number. The sceptical supernaturalism, moreover, had produced no beneficial results. It never built a hospital or a college; it never remodelled a human character; it never constructed any respectable form of human society. The Biblical supernaturalism, beyond all dispute, has made the world better. Yet Owen, the philanthropist, who really desired to promote the physical well-being of men, chose the former and rejected the latter. If this is not credulity of the extreme type, tell us what is.

Faith in the Biblical miracle is more easy and natural than faith in the human supernaturalism, or "spiritualism" as it is called. That a being like Jesus Christ, so pure, so holy, so elevated in his spirit, so benignant in his feelings and so beneficent in his actions, should work a miracle is highly probable. The miracle seems natural to him. We should be surprised, if he never by any act or word had shown that he was connected with a higher world than this. But that Mohammed, for example, a man so cruel and bloody in war, and so lustful in life, should have supernatural power over matter and physical life is utterly improbable. It is unnatural to suppose that wickedness should possess omnipotence. "Can a devil open the eyes of the blind?" John 10:21.

There is still another reason why faith in the human supernaturalism is mere credulity. That there should be supernatural power exerted in Philadelphia in the year 1874 by a circle of men and women is altogether improbable, because there has been no preparation for it. There have been no antecedents like prophecy and pre-announced miracles. It is not a part of a system. It is isolated. It is like lightning from a clear sky which, though abstractly possible, is yet very rare and improbable. The supernaturalism of Christianity was prepared for and expected for long years. The whole line of Jewish history looked towards the incarnation of the Son of God, and the miracles of the Jewish Messiah. Prophecy had foretold it, and even the vague expectations of paganism were waiting for the Desire of all nations. When, therefore, a man like Owen puts confidence in this unheralded supernaturalism, and rejects that which has been foretold and prepared for, he is acting the part of a credulous dupe. Simeon and Anna, like all the spiritual readers and students of the Old Testament, had been waiting for the Consolation of Israel; but Owen and others like him did not stand expecting for many long years the fulfilment of an antecedent prophecy, in the outburst of the supernaturalism which they believed themselves to have witnessed. There was no reason why they should expect it. There had been no communication from God through prophets announcing the coming miracle, and there had been no miraculous line of events going before. The faith of Owen in such circumstances was sheer credulity. It had no ground in history, no support in preceding events. No wonder that instead of the *nunc dimittis* there was the dreadful eclipse of insanity.

INFIDELITY SEEKS A SIGN FROM HEAVEN

The amount and kind of evidence for the truth of the Christian religion depends upon the will of its Author, and not upon the will of man. It is for God to say how many miracles shall be wrought to evince the credibility of the gospel, and it is not for the ruined creature for whose deliverance the gospel is provided, to demand more miracles than have been worked. If the evidences of divine revelation were to be made to depend upon the wishes and caprices of men, miracles would of necessity become the natural order of things, for every generation would clamor for its own portion, and every man would insist upon an ocular demonstration for himself. The Deity would thus be made subject to all the unbelief and hardness of heart so natural to apostate human nature, and would be forced to wait upon his sceptical creatures as a servant upon the master. The sovereignty and majesty of God would be overthrown, and instead of that august Being "who giveth not account of any of his matters," there would be a deity, if such he might be called, who would be continually giving an account, and always standing in an apologetic attitude.

This is the attitude in which such sceptics as Rénan and Tyndall would place the Supreme Ruler of the universe. The French unbeliever insists that, in order that the present generation may have sufficient reason for believing the gospel narrative of the resurrection of Lazarus, the miracle should be repeated. A committee of the French Institute should be appointed, who should examine the corpse to be scientifically certain that it is really a corpse; then the resurrection should be performed in presence of the committee, and such other witnesses as they should appoint, in order that there might be no sleight of hand, and then the report of the savans should be communicated to the public. The English materialist, in a different form, makes a similar proposition. The efficacy of prayer isto be tested by the experiment of praying for the patients in one hospital, and not praying for those of another, both hospitals meanwhile, employing the same physicians and the same mode of treatment. If those who are in the first-mentioned hospital are healed, and those in the second are not, prayer, says Mr. Tyndall, will be proved to be efficacious. But should this actually be the result, should all in the first-mentioned hospital be cured, this would be the performance of a miracle in answer to prayer. This proposition, therefore, of Tyndall is in reality a demand that God work another miracle in addition to those he has previously wrought. The fact that it is to be wrought in answer to the prayers of Christians, instead of in answer to the demand of an unbeliever like Rénan, makes no difference in the principle that is involved. Both proposals alike imply that God shall give additional evidence of the truth of his revelation *whenever it is demanded*, and that the amount and kind of it is to be determined by the creature rather than the Creator.

The spirit that prompts such demands upon God for more miraculous proof of his truth than he has already given, is not a new thing under the sun. A personage of some distinction exhibited it, when he said to Jesus Christ upon the pinnacle of the temple: "If thou be the Son of God, cast thyself down, for it is written, He shall give his angels charge concerning thee, and in their hands they shall bear thee up, lest thou dash thy foot against a stone." This was a demand, made by Satan, in a roundabout manner, through the Messiah, that God work a miracle in proof of the divinity of the gospel. The same spirit animated those Pharisees who "began to question with Christ, seeking of him a sign from heaven, tempting him." Mark 8:11. The unbelieving "brethren" of our Lord were actuated by this same unbelieving temper, which lusts after more miracles and stronger proofs than God is pleased to give to his creatures, when they said to him, "Depart hence, and go into Judea, that thy disciples also may see the works that thou doest. If thou do these things, show thyself to the world." John 7:3-5. And the same spirit flamed out at the crucifixion of the Son of God, when the "chief priests, mocking him, with the scribes and elders, said, He saved others; himself he cannot save. If he be the King of Israel let him now come down from the cross, and we will believe in him." Matt. 27:41, 42. These enemies of Christ, standing beneath the cross, made the same promise that the modern enemies of Christ are making: "Give us another miracle, and we will believe the gospel. Furnish us more evidence of the truth of Christianity, and we will accept it."

The manner in which Jesus Christ treated such demands for more miraculous proofs of the divinity of his mission shows the nature of the demand, and his estimate of it. In the instance of the Satanic proposal, he repelled it with a quotation from the Word of God. In the instance of the Pharisaic demand, "He sighed deeply in his spirit, and saith, Why doth this generation seek after a sign? Verily, I say unto you, there shall no sign be given unto this generation." And when the last demand of this kind was made, as he hung upon the cross, he gave no answer, and his silence was more significant than even his words could have been.

The root of this requisition upon God for more evidence than he has been pleased to give of the truth of Christianity is pronged. It has two forks. One is unbelief, and the other is irreverence. Men are inclined to doubt the gospel from a variety of motives, the chief of which is a dislike of its purity. This inclination they take no pains to weaken, but, on the contrary, they strengthen it, some by their studies, and some by their practices. In this state of mind they clamor for more proof, although they have not fairly weighed the amount of evidence already furnished. And coupled with this is an irreverent spirit. They are not impressed by the Divine majesty. They forget their insignificance and nothingness when compared with God, and presume to dictate the mode and manner in which he shall authenticate his revelation to mankind.

The claim that every age should have new miracles in proof of the Christian religion, would be like the claim that every age should have the right to reopen a case which was settled in court in a past age, upon sufficient testimony. It is a maxim in law, that a criminal shall be tried for an offence only once. If testimony sufficent to acquit him has been presented at his trial, and he is acquitted, this ends the matter. He is dismissed as an innocent person forever after. In like manner, testimony for the truth of the Biblical miracles cannot be continually furnished during all time. It must come from the original eye-witnesses and from them only. It would be absurd to attempt to manufacture new eye-witnesses. And such is the absurdity, when Rénan and Tyndall demand that the miraculous evidence for the divinity of Christianity which accompanied its beginning should be repeated to meet their doubts, and that they, in this way, should be made additional eye-witnesses, and so fall into the same class with the prophets and apostles as attestors to the truth of the Christian religion. "Non tali auxilio, nec defensoribus istis, tempus eget." Stillingfleet (Origines Sacræ, Bk. II. Ch. x.) thus argues against the demand of the infidel that new miracles shall be wrought to overcome his unbelief: "The truth of God's testimony to his revelation was sufficiently sealed at the time of the delivery of it, and is conveyed down in a certain way to us. Is it not sufficient that the charter of a corporation had the prince's broad seal in the time of giving it, but that every succession of men in that corporation must have a new broad seal, or else they ought to question their patent? What ground can there be for that, when the original seal and patent is preserved, and is certainly conveyed down from age to age? So, I say, it is as to us. God's grand charter of grace and mercy to the world through Jesus Christ, was sealed by Divine miracles at the delivery of it to the world; the original patent, namely, the Scriptures, wherein the charter is contained, is conveyed in a most certain manner to us; to this patent the seal is annexed, and in it are contained those undoubted miracles which were wrought in confirmation of it; so that a new sealing of this patent is wholly needless, unless we have some cause of suspicion that the original patent itself were lost, or that the first sealing was not true. If the latter, then the Christian religion is not true if the miracles wrought for confirmation of it were false; because the truth of it depends so much on the verity and divinity of the miracles which were then wrought. If the first be suspected, namely, the certain conveyance of the patent, namely, the Scriptures, some sure grounds for such a suspicion must be produced by the sceptic in a matter of such great moment, especially when the great and numerous societies of the Christian world do all concur unanimously in the contrary."

THE HASTY INFERENCES OF INFIDELITY

In the recent attempt to prove that the human race have a much longer antiquity than the Bible teaches, great ignorance of very common and well-established sources of information is sometimes exhibited. The reader of any of the usual histories which describe savage or semi-civilized races often finds that the use of stone in lieu of iron or other metals, is a custom that does not imply very great antiquity in the rude population so employing it. The American Indian, at the time of the first settlement of the United States, still shaped the flint into arrow-heads and spear-heads. His ancestors before him had done so from time immemorial; but that time immemorial, in the instance of the Indian, would not run back, probably, so far as the age in which Herodotus wrote. For all the indications go to show that the Western continent was not peopled until after the Eastern had been over-populated. But the modern theorist, in his eagerness to prove the untrustworthiness of Scripture, would have us believe that the stone age, as he calls it, antedates all history, both secular and sacred.

We have been interested in a curious refutation of this which is furnished by the historian Gibbon—a writer who certainly cannot be charged with partiality for revealed truth, or any desire to establish it upon an unassailable foundation. Readers of the recent treatises upon the antiquity of man, will remember how much is made of the so-called *lacustrine* dwellings. In Switzerland, and other parts of Europe, remains have been discovered, at the outlets or inlets of lakes, of piles driven into the morass, and of the huts which were built upon them. The inhabitants seem to have been a rude and savage race who dwelt partly upon the land, and partly upon the water, and so constructed their dwellings that they might have ready access to either. They may have adopted this method as the first founders of Venice did, in order to be secure from the attacks of their enemies from the land. Or they might have wished to render the taking of fish, which was their principal food, more easy. Many reasons might be conjectured for such a species of habitation, and no one, certainly, would have seen in such a phenomenon any evidence of a pre-Adamite life antedating all history. Even at the present day, there are tribes in Eastern Asia and in South America who adopt the very same method, in order to escape the inconveniences of those inundations which overflow vast tracts of alluvial territory.

In the forty-second chapter of the *Decline and Fall*, Gibbon describes the incursion of the Bulgarians, or, as they have been more popularly called, the Huns, into the regions this side of the Danube. Before entering upon the description of their devastating march, he gives some account of their manners and way of life in their home on the plains of Russia, Lithuania, and Poland. He tells us that " four thousand six hundred villages were scattered over the provinces of Russia and Poland, and their huts were hastily built of rough timber, in a country deficient both in stone and iron. Erected, or rather concealed, in the depth of forests, on the banks of rivers, or the edge of morasses, we may not perhaps without flattery compare them to the architecture of the beaver; which they resembled in a double issue to the land and water, for the escape of the savage inhabitant, an animal less cleanly, less diligent, and less social than that marvellous quadruped." Now this will answer equally well for the description of the Swiss lake dwellings, which have been cited in proof that there was a primitive man in the heart of Europe long before Adam was made out of the dust of the ground. The lacustrine dwellings of the Bulgarian Sclaves were almost identically the same with those of the dwellers among the Alps. Nay, the builders of the Swiss structures very possibly may have been descendants of those Huns who when they crossed the Danube were never entirely driven back to their old home in Russia. But Gibbon attributes no very great antiquity to these barbarous men. The incursion over the Danube, which he describes, began in the reign of Justinian, who died A. D. 565.

Some three or four centuries may be allowed for their residence in Russia previous to the overpopulation which impelled them to move westward, and then we should not be forced backward into time even as far as the advent of our Lord. This is the reckoning and chronology of Edward Gibbon; a scholar with whose learning that of a writer like Lubbock is not to be compared for a moment.

The characteristic of the recent attack upon the credibility of Scripture history is, hasty inference from ill-understood facts. There is ignorance or else superficial knowledge in the start, and then a headlong deduction which is inspired more by the wish of the theorist than by calm reason. That a race of barbarians should live in huts built upon piles, was for the mind of Gibbon no such very extraordinary phenomenon in the history of man as to suggest that it must have been a race different from any that have lived since the historical period. He never dreamed of postulating an immense antiquity for it. But a theorizer who has a point to carry, finds in it evidence sufficient to overthrow the chronology of Revelation, which is the chronology of Christian literature and science, in distinction from Pagan and Infidel.

STEREOTYPED ERRORS OF INFIDELITY

A PERIODICAL circulating among mechanics and artisans, in a recent number, contains an article in the interest of infidelity, which reiterates certain misstatements that have been made so long that the correction of them seems to be useless. The writer says that the strife between conservatism and progress has been going on from time immemorial. The former is represented by theology, the later by science. Science has been opposed by theology, and the following illustrations are given:

1. "There was a time when the whole human race considered our earth to be a flat, and to consist of three connected continents, Europe, Asia and Africa. The ancient astronomers who announced the rotundity of the earth were contradicted by the theological priests. But ultimately science prevailed, and conservative theology had to acknowledge that it had been wrong." The erroneous geography which the writer describes is that of Homer and Herodotus. There is no evidence that either of these authors came in conflict

with "astronomers who announced the rotundity of the earth," or that the pagan priests did. This theory was held generally in Greece and Rome without molestation. But the writer probably refers to the modern discussions respecting the sphericity of the earth. In this instance, there was a difference of opinion upon both sides. Some of the theologians agreed with some of the astronomers in thinking that the old geography was erroneous; and some of the astronomers themselves agreed with some of the theologians in holding to the old view. Neither the "conservatism" nor the "progress" was all upon one side. The doctrine of the rotundity of the earth was the result of a great discussion in which all the learned took a part, and until the matter was settled beyond dispute there was as much heated debate amongst the astronomers as amongst the theologians.

2. "Next came the doctrine of the motion of the earth." The writer, of course, weeps the customary tear over Galileo. Though the doctrine "was condemned as ungodly by the whole Christian priesthood, Protestant as well as Roman Catholic, and this good man was compelled to swear to the falsehoods of the priests, yet progressive science was again victorious over conservative theology." The Protestant church had nothing at all to do with the persecution of Galileo. And the Papal church as a whole cannot be said to have taken ground against him. It was a quarrel between a party in that church and Galileo.

He had offended the Jesuits, and this influential body in the Italian diocese, it is true, attempted to force his opinions. But in France and Germany, there was much agreement with Galileo in the scientific circles of the Papal church. He had adopted the views of Copernicus, who is the real father of the modern astronomy, and not Galileo. The views of Copernicus had already obtained considerable currency in Papal Europe. This great genius, who refuted the Ptolemaic astronomy and announced that which goes under his name, and which Galileo adopted from him, lived and died in the Papal church. He published his great work at the urgent request of a Papal cardinal, and dedicated it by permission to the Pope himself (Paul III.). That it should meet with opposition from some of the astronomers and theologians was to be expected. A new theory cannot be adopted by everybody at once. But Copernicus was not persecuted in the least by the Papal see, and the Protestant church was just coming into existence when his work was published in 1543.

3. "Afterwards," continues the writer, "came the doctrine of the great antiquity of the earth, which geology compelled the theologians to concede, who previously held that the globe was only six thousand years old, and was made in six days." The theologians were in advance of the physicists here. Augustine, long before the time of geology, interpreted the first chapter of Genesis as teaching an original creation of chaotic matter, ages upon

ages ago, and then its subsequent formation and arrangement in the six days' work, which he denominated "God-divided days," or periods. Origen, still earlier than Augustine, went so far as to hold to an eternal creation of the universe, which would make it older than even the geologists make it.

4. Next, this advocate of science versus theology asserts "that there is evidence that man has existed at least one hundred thousand years upon the earth," and that theology will be forced to yield this point, though it has not yet done it. Upon this, we have two remarks to make. First, the theologian is not persecuting the physicist for his statement. We have not heard that anybody has been burnt at the stake for holding this view. Secondly, the evidence, at the present writing, that man has existed one hundred thousand years upon the earth, is infinitesimal. That there will be sufficient found hereafter to demonstrate the fact, and that the theologian will be forced to admit it, is only a prophecy. But there is no logic against prophecy. We cannot reason with a soothsayer.

And finally, the writer assures his readers that the doctrine of evolution is destined to overthrow the theological doctrines of a difference between mind and matter, and of an original perfection in man and a subsequent fall and degradation. This, too, like the preceding, is vaticination, and might be dismissed as such. In respect, however, to the alleged fact of the development of inorganic into organic matter, of the non-vital into the vital, and of animal sensation into thought, we will close with a single remark. If evolution really is a law and process of nature, it ought to be as uniform and invariable as any other law and process, say gravitation, and there ought to be thousands and millions of instances of it. But as yet there is not a single solitary instance. Darwin's pigeons are pigeons still. A mere theory, which has for its support nothing in the least degree approximating to the uniformity and universality that are demanded and exhibited in the instance of acknowledged laws of nature, is not scientific, but ridiculous. Any real and actual law of nature cannot be put under a bushel. It must show itself upon a grand scale, as constantly going on. Instead, therefore, of being compelled to ransack all nature for an instance in which one *real* species has developed into another real species, and not finding a single instance, the "scientist" ought to have found the instances crowding and multiplying upon him. Before he broached a theory which is as revolutionary and destructive of all past science as red republicanism is of social order, he ought to have discovered at least a few instances in which the grain of sand becomes vital protoplasm ; in which the vegetable seed becomes the egg of animal life ; in which the anthropoid ape is transformed into a human being.

THE EFFRONTERY OF INFIDELITY

The friend and biographer of Strauss describes the *Glaubenslehre* of this writer as doing for Christianity what the balance-sheet does for a mercantile firm. It shows what the assets are; how much the concern is actually worth after the bad debts and depreciated or damaged goods are subtracted. The Christian religion, according to Strauss, contains a good many legendary materials like the monkish chronicles of the middle ages, a good many contradictions, and a great many statements contrary to reason and the five senses, and to physical science. It is the business of a philosopher to sift out this chaff and show the few kernels of wheat that are left. Christianity contains some grains of truth, and it is the object of Strauss's critique to exhibit them.

It is not necessary to say that Strauss's balance-sheet shows but few assets for the religion of Christ, as it is presented in the four Gospels. This widespread religion, which has so unaccountably succeeded in getting the globe under its intellectual and moral influence, is substantially bankrupt.

But how is the balance-sheet to be made out? Much depends upon this. In determining the value of depreciated stock, the merchant has an undisputed and certain rule of measurement. The current price at which it sells in market is a guide which all parties will accept. By what measuring rule does our critic estimate the assets of Christianity? Has he one that is as trustworthy and accurate as that of the mercantile cashier?

According to Zeller (the biographer of whom we have spoken), Strauss adopts the Hegelian philosophy as "the rule and measure" by which everything in the Christian religion is to be tested and tried. He has no doubts about the credibility of Hegelianism. His faith in this German, whose breath was in his nostrils, being born in 1770 and dying in 1831, is implicit. He does not begin his examination of Christianity by first demonstrating the trustworthiness of the rule of measurement which he is going to use, but he assumes this as axiomatic and indisputable.

We have here an instance of the remarkable effrontery of infidelity. Upon presenting himself before the public, the opponent of the infallibility of Jesus Christ begins by asking the public to concede the infallibility of George William Frederick Hegel. Nothing is scientific, says Strauss, but the Absolute and Unconditioned. Every system must be tested, not by relative and partial truth, but by the pure reason itself freed from all prejudice and prepossessions. We must not look at Christianity in the light of our moral intuitions, of our education at our mothers' knees, or of our personal needs and wants in times of sorrow or fear. The mere feelings of men, women, and children are no test of the truth of a system. We must dismiss all feeling, and look at the four Gospels with a calm and dispassionate intellect. We must judge Christianity by an absolute standard.

And this absolute standard is the Hegelian philosophy. Our readers perhaps will think that we are hardly doing justice to a writer who has made so much noise in the world as David Frederick Strauss. Such a barefaced begging of the question, they will think, he could not be guilty of. But we assure them that there is no misrepresentation here. Hegel, without any word of explanation or attempt to justify the postulate, is set up in the very beginning as the authority by which Christianity is to be tested. He is to make out the balance-sheet, and determine what the assets really are. His system of philosophy is the sum and result of all anterior systems, containing all that is true in them, and excluding all that is false, and is so far in advance of them all as to be the solution of all problems, and the key to all knowledge. This is what is claimed for the philosophy in question. And Strauss, who cannot believe a miracle, can believe this. Ask him if Jesus Christ is omniscient, and holds the key of all knowledge, as well as the keys of death and hell, and he answers, No. Ask him who does hold the key, and he replies that Hegel does. Hegel is in effect the Absolute, because he is the author of the philosophy of the Absolute.

It is pleasant to be informed. There has been much inquiry respecting the Absolute. Some have denied that there is any such idea or reality. Others have asserted that there is, but that it cannot be known. The question is settled by Strauss. He who knew the Absolute lived in Berlin, and was professor in the university there.

It is difficult to treat such a claim as this of Strauss, in respect to Hegelianism, with seriousness. With all his errors, that remarkable and powerful thinker who has given his name to the most closely concatenated system in modern history, would never have thought of setting up such a claim. His own attitude toward Christ and Christianity, though not that of Newton or Pascal, was far from being like that of Strauss. He never arrogated so much for himself. It is the height of absurdity, to set up human reason as it exists in a single individual man as the measure and test of all truth, Christianity included. The elder and more respectable Rationalists never did this. They maintained, it is true, that reason is the test of all truth, but then it was reason as found in a multitude of men, and not in one man only. They would appeal to the *consensus* of reason, as seen in various systems, and in all ages. But Strauss is much less reasonable than Rationalism, in placing all truth at the mercy of one human mind, and a single human system.

The proper feeling toward such a claim as that made by Strauss, in his critique of Christianity, is that of contempt. When a single human intellect is proposed as the infallible norm and test, and the demand is made that we subject our views of Christ and Christianity to it, we take a lesson from the old East Indians. When Alexander the Great was overrunning India, he sent messengers to a certain Indian tribe, demanding that they acknowledge him to be a god. The sturdy savages sent back the contemptuous answer: "If Alexander wants to be a god, let him be a god."

THE MEANNESS OF INFIDELITY

It is reported that a celebrated infidel once said that if St. Paul should personally and upon his word of honor assure him that the gospel is true, he would believe him, "for," said he, "St. Paul was such a gentleman!" We believe that Christianity can accept this compliment. The Christian is the highest style of man, and of course he is a gentleman. "Be courteous," is one of the injunctions of Scripture. But Christianity cannot return the compliment to Infidelity. From some cause or other, scepticism is lacking in that sincere, upright, and honorable spirit which lies at the foundation of a gentlemanly nature.

We have had this fact forced upon our notice in reading the autobiography of the late John Stuart Mill, and we propose to mention some particulars that illustrate it. The father of John Mill was James Mill, the author of the *History of British India*. He was the son of a Scotch Presbyterian, and when a boy was recommended by his abilities to the notice of a nobleman whose wife had established a fund in the University of Edinburgh for educating young men for the Scottish Church. James Mill "went through the usual course of study and was licensed as a preacher, but never followed the profession, having satisfied himself that he could not believe the doctrines of that or any other church." Through his whole after life he was a disbeliever not merely of the truths of Christianity, but of those of natural religion. The creed of the deist, who believes in the existence of a God, and in the distinction between right and wrong, was more than he could adopt. His son tells us that his position was as nearly that of atheism as anything. He taught that son that religion is not merely a "mental delusion," but a "great moral evil." He impressed upon the recipient mind of his child, "that the manner in which the world came into existence is a subject on which nothing is known; that the question, Who made me? cannot be answered, because we have no experience or authentic information from which to answer it; and that any answer only throws the difficulty a step further back, since the question immediately presents itself, Who made God?" What we wish to bring into distinct notice, in connection with this infidelity, is the fact that the education which enabled James Mill to obtain a respectable position in the East India House, and which laid the foundation of his success in life, as well as that of his son after him, was given to him by Christianity. He was started in life by the funds of devout piety, and he was afterward maintained in life by the patronage of an institution which, to say the least, was nominally Christian. Yet he never acknowledged this indebtedness to a religion which he rejected and reviled. It is fair to suppose that if the elder Mill, after the decided change in his views from belief to infidelity, had felt himself in honor bound to return the amount which he had received from an endowment devoted to the preparation of students for the Scottish Church, and had so done, his son would have mentioned the fact. This is an illustration of what we call the meanness of infidelity.

Again, we learn from this autobiography that the elder Mill taught the younger to conceal his scepticism, in order not to injure his worldly prospects. "In giving me an opinion contrary to that of the world, my father," he says, "thought it necessary to give it as one which could not prudently be avowed to the world." The son thinks that this was attended with some disadvantages, but the absence of a sincere reverence for what is believed to be truth, and a readiness to die if need be for it, is not mentioned as one of them. Indeed, he apologizes for his father's concealment of his infidel opinions, because at that day they were exceedingly unpopular. But at the present time, he says, "the great advance in liberty of discussion has greatly altered the moralities of the question," and he thinks that his father, if living now, would not practice or inculcate the concealment of sceptical opinions, "unless in the cases, becoming fewer every day, in which frankness on these subjects would either risk the loss of the means of subsistence, or would amount to exclusion from some sphere of usefulness peculiarly suitable to the capacities of the individual" (Autobiography, p. 45). The son acted afterward upon this principle when he became a candidate for Parliament. He frankly answered all questions respecting his political views, but announced from the beginning that he would answer no questions relating to his religious opinions. If John Stuart Mill had been as explicit upon the hustings in his denunciation of the religion and morals that have made England what it is, as he is in some paragraphs of this Autobiography, his election, even by the highly-excited and radical constituency that placed him in Parliament for a brief season, would have been impossible. And this he well knew.

We do not think that there is in all literature a more repulsive instance of a mean and sordid infidelity, than is presented in this Autobiography. And the writer does not even dream of being ashamed of it. His moral sense has, by the operation of his godless creed, become so obtuse that what a high-minded and gentlemanly nature, not to speak of a solemn and earnest religious spirit, would shrink from as degrading, he coolly and without a blush describes as belonging to himself, and as being one of his principles of action.

THE CONNECTION BETWEEN INFIDELITY AND SENSUALITY

Richard Baxter makes the following remark respecting himself: "I observed, easily, in myself, that if at any time Satan did more than at other times weaken my belief of Scripture and the life to come, my zeal in religious duty abated with it, and I grew more indifferent in religion than before." This good man found that infidelity is favorable to sin, and that in proportion as doubt concerning God and the Bible rises, religion declines. But if this is true of the renewed man, it is still more so of the unrenewed; and it is in this latter reference that we would say a word.

The two truths that are doubted and denied by the current infidelity are those very two which Baxter mentions: First, the credibility of the Scriptures, and second, the reality of another world than this in which we are now living. If a man is infidel upon these two points, he cannot be religious, either logically or practically. For it would be absurd for a man to live with reference to another world, if he does not believe that there is one, or to govern his conduct by a book which he denies to be trustworthy. Perhaps it will be replied that a man may do right because it is right, whether there is a God or not, whether there be another world or not. This is the sublimated piety suggested by Strauss, who charges upon Christian virtue the defect of being selfish, in having so much reference to God and a future existence. Man, he says, ought to be righteous for righteousness sake, and not because another Being has commanded him to be so, or because there is another world in which this righteousness will make him happy. But such virtue as this, in the first place, is self-contradictory. Righteousness supposes a standard or rule. What rule? Whose rule? Righteousness without a God and without a law is inconceivable. And in the second place such virtue as this is impracticable. Mankind have never dreamed of working righteousness in this abstract style. They reason with St. Paul: "If in this life, only, we have hope in Christ, we are of all men most miserable. What advantageth it me, if the dead rise not? Let us eat and drink, for to-morrow we die." When Strauss attempts to be more religious than St. Paul, and complains that the apostle's virtue is not sufficiently exalted for him, we too turn infidel, and doubt his sincerity. Macaulay describes one of Southey's heroes as marked by contrary tempers; being at one time all clay, at another all spirit. In the former mood, he "makes love like cattle." In the latter mood, he "makes love like the seraphim, and is too ethereal to be married." This Don Roderic in his spiritual mood is much like a man who is too religious to be a Christian.

But Strauss has a motive in thus asking for a better virtue than the Christian, or a purer charity than that of Howard. He desires to overthrow belief in the existence of God and the infallibility of the Bible, well knowing that men will never practice such sublimated ethics as he speaks of, but will plunge into worldliness and sensuality in order to get all the enjoyment they can before they rot into unconsciousness by evolution.

There are degrees, however, in infidelity; but its influence is the same in kind. It is sensualizing, be it moderate or be it extreme. A man may not deny all the doctrines of the Bible, or all of the attributes of God. He may select some and reject the remainder. There is much scepticism of this sort. But the individual will in every instance be guided in his choice by his epicurean inclination rather than by his moral conscience. Is it probable that he will select the strict doctrines and attributes, and reject the others? Will he affirm that God is a consuming fire, but deny that God is love? Will he accept the doctrine of endless punishment, but reject that of the resurrection of the body? No; his unbelief will retain those truths that present little opposition to a life of pleasure in this world, and will cast out those that stand directly in the way of it. But in assenting to some of the truths of revelation and discarding some, the man in question is as really infidel in spirit as Hume or Strauss, upon the principle that he who breaks the law in one point, is guilty of law-breaking.

This connection between infidel opinions and sinful practice, noticed by the devout Baxter, should be kept in view. If men would remember that if they do anything to weaken their belief in the Word of God and the reality of another life, they thereby remove a positive restraint upon their appetites and passions and promote sensuality, either refined or gross, they would be likely to think twice before doing it. They would be more careful in regard to the books that they read, and the teachers they listen to. Instead of toiling and studying to weaken their orthodoxy, they would toil and study to strengthen it. They would at least endeavor to keep their head level, as the phrase is.

THE INFIDEL PHYSICS

WHY is there so much infidelity among the naturalists of the present generation ? The answer to this question may be found in the distinction which Whewell makes between inductive and deductive habits of mind. In his valuable Bridgewater treatise upon "Astronomy and General Physics considered with Reference to Natural Theology," this learned man of science shows that the ascent, by induction, from particular facts and phenomena to a general law that shall connect and explain them all, is favorable to the idea of a First Cause, while the descent by deduction, from a general law to the innumerable applications of it, is not so favorable, and perhaps is unfavorable. When the great discoverers, like Copernicus, Galileo, Kepler, Newton, Boyle, and Pascal, are employed in reducing to law and order the complex facts of the material world, they go up from one generalization to another, and from one law to another. One cause is resolved into another yet more powerful, and this into a third, and so on until they reach the limits of their science. In this way, the idea of a *higher* cause is kept continually before them, and this does not allow them to stop until they reach a First Cause. "The business of natural philosophy," says Newton, "is to argue from phenomena without feigning hypotheses, and to deduce causes from effects, till we come to the very first cause, which certainly is not a mechanical one." And it is a fact which ought not to be forgotten in these days when sceptical naturalists are so self-conceited, that all the great scientific geniuses who have made epochs in natural science by discovering new laws have been believers in revelation, and many of them devout experimental Christians.

But when the process is reversed, and the naturalist begins to go down instead of up, we do not find so much original genius, nor do we find so much religious reverence and faith. After Kepler had discovered the law which connects the periodic times with the diameters of the planetary orbits, and Newton had discovered the law of universal gravitation according to the inverse square of the distance, it was then comparatively easy, and required far less of original intellectual power, to deduce, or manufacture, inferences and conclusions from these laws. The natural philosopher of this species was not employed in searching for the first cause. On the contrary, he assumed that he had the first cause in the law, and was busy looking for its effects. The great law of gravitation, he said, is the prime cause of the motions of the heavenly bodies, and he spent his life and employed much acute talent in showing mathematically how the law operates. In this way, the laws of nature are thrust in the place of the First Cause. Some of the distinguished mathematicians who have reasoned from the premises furnished them by Kepler and Newton, and have developed by means of algebra and the calculus what is contained in them, have been unbelievers in greater or less degree. D'Alembert, Laplace, and Lagrange, are examples. But there is no necessity that the deductive habit of mind should be sceptical. There is no need of assuming that the force of gravitation is itself the First Cause. D'Alembert and Laplace should have said as Newton, its discoverer, said: "The business of natural philosophy is to deduce causes from effects, till we come to the very first cause, which certainly is not a mechanical one." But, instead of this, when they reached the great and universal law which regulates all the movements of the material universe, they followed Newton no further, and, as the idolatrous Israelites did to the golden calf, bowed down to a mere blind and unconscious, though exceedingly mathematical force, and said: "This is God; this is the cause of causes."

Now, this same tendency to deduction is making infidels of naturalists in this generation. Science, compared with what it was as cultivated by Kepler and Newton, is now very contracted in its range. The energy, we might say the rage of the naturalist's mind, is now expended upon biology and geology. Formerly, the great mathematical sciences of astronomy, optics, mechanics, and hydrostatics, enlisted the chief attention. These are now in the background; and the names which are most in the popular mouth, and the fugitive literature, are those of Darwin, Huxley, Tyndall, and the like. Philosophers of this species cannot be classed with Newton, Pascal, Euler, and Laplace, in respect to intellectual power. They are not mathematicians, like Herschel and Whewell. Probably, not one of them has read through the *Principia* and the *Mécanique Céleste*. But they have fastened upon some general principles discovered by greater and more reverent minds than theirs, have postulated these as the ultimate fact, and have gone on making deductions and forming theories which "untenant creation of its God," and deify matter and material forces.

It has been truly said that the mark of a philosophical mind is to seek for a first cause, and not to be content with a second cause. Tried by this test, the devotees of the current infidel physics are not philosophers. Is it philosophical to assert that the brain is the first cause of thought, merely because in our limited experience on earth no mind thinks without a brain? Is it philosophical to put the second occasional cause for the first efficient cause, and say that the brain is the mind? Because there is phosphorus in the human brain, is it philosophical to contend that phosphorus is the indispensable condition of all thought in the universe, and that where there is no phosphorus there is no thought? Do not God and the angels think? These questions might be asked indefinitely, in regard to the many assertions without proof in the current materialism.

What is the remedy? A wider and deeper science, greater familiarity with the dii majorum gentium, the scientific geniuses who discovered these laws of nature, and who understood their relation to the Author of nature far better than do the empirics and sciolists who are misusing and abusing their discoveries. There will be no new and original addition to the stock of scientific knowledge, until the inductive habit of mind is restored. Men must once more acknowledge and worship the First Cause, and no longer deify secondary occasional causes, if the science of nature is to make progress. There has been a generation of such naturalists, or "scientists" as they are inelegantly called, but what great discovery has been made by them? There have been applications of old laws and forces; but who of this class has had any new intuition into the secrets of nature? Is Darwin's truism, that those animals which are best fitted to survive do survive and propagate with more or less variation, a wonderful discovery in physics? The remainder of his theory, that the variation results in the origination of a new species, is not a discovery but only an hypothesis, because the proof is wanting.

MODERN APOCRYPHAL GOSPELS

There are a number of spurious narratives relating to Jesus Christ which go under the name of the Apocryphal Gospels. They contain some of the elements of the four canonical Gospels, but are made up to a great extent of fanciful stories which the imagination of a later time than that of the apostles invented. In many instances, a miracle is described and attributed to our Lord which bears some resemblance to one or more of the genuine ones. In the so-called Gospel of Thomas, for example, it is related that when Jesus was a boy of five years, while playing upon the Sabbath-day with his mates, he made twelve sparrows out of some clay. These playmates informed Joseph, his father, that his son "had taken clay and made sparrows of it, which it was unlawful to do upon the Sabbath-day." Joseph asks Jesus why he has done this, and rebukes him for the breach of the Sabbath. Jesus releases the sparrows, saying, "Fly into the sky; no one shall ever kill you." The sparrows flew up into the heavens praising God Almighty.

Some of these Apocryphal Gospels are less extravagant than others; but all of them lack the simplicity, naturalness, and what may be called the honest good sense of the canonical Gospels. The miracles attributed to our Saviour in these spurious records are odd, capricious, and oftentimes puerile. They seem to be performed for the purpose of causing wonder and admiration, like the tricks of a juggler, and not for the purpose of attesting some divine truth or solemn declaration of God.

These legendary and spurious narratives have never been regarded with respect or confidence even by the most credulous and superstitious portions of Christendom. The Papal church, though accepting the Old Testament Apocrypha, had too much sense and discrimination to place the Apocryphal Gospels in the canon. The consequence is, that these productions are about as unknown and obsolete a portion of literature as can be mentioned. No one has ever built a theory upon them; and no one has gone to them to derive either the doctrine or the person of Jesus Christ. They have died from utter contempt, and are as dead as a door-nail.

But there are some modern Apocryphal Gospels which have received some attention from a certain class in modern times, and yet have no more claims to respect and belief than the ancient. We refer to such fanciful and imaginative productions as the Gospel of Strauss and the Gospel of Rénan. These too have a resemblance to the four Gospels, and could not have been composed without their aid. These too, like the old Gospel of Thomas, or of Nicodemus, or of James, are the genuine Gospels modified to suit the individual notions of the new "Gospeller." The earlier forgers thought that the narratives of Matthew, Mark, Luke and John had not miracles enough, and accordingly they invented some new ones, and added them. The later forgers thought that the four evangelists had introduced too many miracles into the account, and accordingly they subtract the miracle altogether. The old cheats of the Patristic period worked over the documents of the four evangelists, and constructed a picture of Jesus Christ which in their opinion was an improvement upon the original picture. The new cheats of the nineteenth century, taking the same old documents, alter and modify them to suit their own tastes and opinions, both philosophical and religious, and have presented the modern world with their portraiture of Jesus Christ, which they assure us is much superior to any preceding one. A vivid but whimsical writer of this generation wrote a book which he entitled *Sartor Resartus:* the Tailor retailored. These Gospels of the ancient Superstition and the modern Unbelief might be called the Evangelium Resartum—the Gospel cut over and patched up. What is the difference between inventing such a story as that of making birds out of clay, which is found in the old legend of Thomas, and inventing such a story as that of Christ's swooning on the cross, and then reviving in the cool tomb, which is found in the new legend of Rénan? It is a pure invention in each instance. The pseudo-Thomas was not an eye-witness of the imaginary miracle which he relates, and never saw a person that was an eye-witness of it. Rénan was not an eye-witness of the imaginary swoon which he relates, and has neither eye-witnesses nor documentary evidence to sustain him. The swoon of Christ is as pure a figment and fiction as any of the wonderful stories told in the *Acta Sanctorum* respecting any saint in the Papal calendar. Rénan and those like him made it up out of their own heads. There is nothing historical in it, because it is not related by any contemporary witness. It is a modern invention. These parallels might be run indefinitely. The so-called Gospel of the Infancy relates the following miracle: Jesus was one day playing with boys of his own age upon the roof of a house, when one of them slipped and fell to the ground and was killed. The rest of the boys ran away in fright. Jesus remained, and when the neighbors came up they accused him of having thrown the dead boy from the roof. He denies the accusation, but is not believed. Whereupon, standing over the dead body, Jesus cries with a loud voice: "Zeno, who threw thee down from the roof?" The dead answered: "It was not thou, Lord, but the evil One who threw me down." The Christian church from the beginning has rejected such a narrative as this, because it has no historical support. No one knows the name of the writer of the Gospel of the

Infancy, and every student knows that it was composed from three to six hundred years after the time of Christ's existence on earth. But there is full as strong reason why the Christian church should reject such a story as that of Rénan respecting the hallucination of Mary Magdalen. This tale of her seeing an apparition, is the invention of a Frenchman who lived in Paris more than eighteen hundred years after Christ. It has no foundation in any document of any kind. Nothing like it is to be found even in those earlier Apocryphal Gospels to which Rationalism is not ashamed sometimes to go, when it finds anything to suit its wishes and purposes.

There is one difference, however, between the Gospel of the pseudo-Thomas and the Gospel of Strauss or the Gospel of Rénan, which is not in favor of the latter. The old romancer wrote out his story. One can begin and read the Gospel of Thomas, or the Gospel of the Infancy, or the Gospel of Nicodemus, through, from beginning to end, and whatever else he may or may not find, he finds a continuous narrative. But the modern romancer tantalizes us. He does not compose his Gospel, but tells us how it should be composed. He is not so interesting as his older brother, because he does not narrate the story of Jesus so that he who runs may *read* it.

Nothing would be more amusing, to say the least, than to have had Strauss sit down and rewrite in Hellenistic Greek the Gospel narrative according to his own theories and views—rejecting all that he thought to be unhistorical, and inserting all that he thought to be historical. We opine that such an Evangelium Apocryphum Straussii, or Evangelium Apocryphum Renanis, would read as curiously as the Evangelium Thomæ, and not so edifyingly as the Protevangelium Jacobi, the best of the Apocryphal Gospels.

THE TWO VIEWS OF THE OLD TESTAMENT

There are two views of the nature of the Old Testament: The Historical or Traditional; and the Rationalistic or Pseudo-Critical. The one is held by the church, the other by parties and individuals, sometimes within the church, and sometimes outside of it.

1. The Historical or Traditional view is: that the books of the Old Testament are the infallible word of God communicated to a small circle selected out of the people of Israel for this purpose. Certain holy men of old spake as they were moved by the Holy Ghost. These books, consequently, do not contain the religious ideas of the uninspired Hebrew race, but the teachings of the Supreme Being. The Old Testament, though Hebrew in language and modes of expression and forms of thought, is not Hebrew literature, but Divine revelation; because literature, properly so called, is the natural and spontaneous product of a national mind. The Old Testament is not the development of the common Hebrew mind as

Greek literature is of the Greek mind, and Latin literature is of the Roman; but it is a special disclosure from the Divine mind made only to a limited number of Hebrews, in order that they might teach the Hebrew people as a whole, and through them teach the whole world, in matters pertaining to religion. The religion of the Old Testament, consequently, is not one of the natural religions of the globe, but a supernatural religion, different from them in kind, intended to enlighten their darkness, correct their errors, and do a work for sinful man which none of them can do.

By reason of its Divine origin, the Old Testament is an independent book. The narratives in Genesis of the creation and fall, of the deluge and of Babel, were not constructed out of the similar accounts that are found in the archives of ancient nations. These latter were not original and older materials wrought into the Mosaic narrative, but later echoes and corruptions of a revelation made by God to Adam concerning events that could have had no human spectator, and of a testimony concerning events that had human spectators like Seth, Enoch, and Noah. The accounts of the creation, fall, and deluge, handed down in the line of Seth and the patriarchs, were finally combined by Moses, under Divine guidance, into a history of primeval man, which has an accuracy and trustworthiness such as belong to no heathen legends or myths.[1]

[1] "The great cause of most of the confusion in the tradition of other nations was the frequent mixing of several families one with another. Now that God might, as it were, satisfy the world of the

Originated in this manner, the Old Testament religion, unlike the natural and national religions of the world, is unmixed and homogeneous in its nature. It is pure monotheism, from first to last; from Genesis to Malachi. From beginning to end, also, it contains the promise and the doctrine of a Redeemer and of Redemption. There is no polytheism nor pantheism, in the religion of Israel as enunciated by Moses and the Prophets. The Hebrew people themselves, from time to time, became more or less idolatrous and sensual, but the religion which Jehovah gave them through inspired persons had nothing of this tincture. In brief, the Old Testament is a revelation, not an evolution; a revelation from the Divine mind, and not an evolution of the Hebrew mind.

2. The Rationalistic or Pseudo-Critical view is: that the books of the Old Testament are the prod-

Israelites' capacity to preserve the tradition entire, he prohibited their mixture by marriages with the people of other nations. So that in Moses' time it was a very easy matter to run up their lineal descent as far as the flood, nay, up to Adam; for Adam conversed sometimes with Lamech, Noah's father; for Lamech was born A.M. 874. Adam died 930; so that fifty-six years, according to that computation, were Adam and Lamech contemporary. Can we think Noah ignorant of the ancient tradition of the world, when his father was so long coævous with Adam; and Methusaleh, his grandfather, who was born A.M. 687, died not till A.M. 1656, according to our learned primate Usher; that is, was six hundred years contemporary with Noah. Then, his son was probably living in some part of Jacob's time, or Isaac's at least; and how easily might the general tradition of the ancient history be continued thence to the time of Moses, when the number of families agreeing in this tradition was increased and incorporated by a common ligament of religion." Stillingfleet: Origines Sacræ, II., ii., 9.

uct of the common Hebrew mind, as this spontaneously developed in a national literature from age to age. The religion of Israel, like the religions of Babylon and Assyria, of Egypt and India, of Greece and Rome, has no uniform and homogeneous character. It begins, it is claimed, like all human religions, in polytheism, and passes gradually upward into monotheism. The religion of Israel was at first idolatrous. Traces of fetishism and polytheism are said to be found in the older parts of the Pentateuch, which is a heterogeneous collection made by several unknown compilers, and of which only a few brief fragments date back of the time of Moses. The religion of the Hebrews at the time of Moses and the Exodus, as shown by later fragments incorporated into the Pentateuch, was not monotheism, but polytheism, like that of Egypt from which they emigrated, and like that of all the surrounding peoples. Gradually the Hebrew religion improves, through that development of the religious sentiment by which man, generally, grows better and better. In the eighth century before Christ it had become a semi-pagan idolatry, partly monotheistic, as is seen from the writings of the prophets, which differ from the Pentateuch in this particular. Jehovah, the national god, who had previously been worshipped under the form of a bullock in both Judah and Israel, began to be conceived of in a more spiritual manner. In the seventh century before Christ the process was complete in a pure monotheism, which ever afterward continued to be the religion of Israel.

This theory supposes that there was no supernatural revelation of religious truth to the Hebrew people, but only that ordinary unfolding of man's religious nature which is common to every nation. The books of the Old Testament are a history of this unfolding in the case of the Hebrews, and are no more infallible and entitled to be the rule of religious faith for all mankind than any other books or literatures which contain similar accounts of national religions. The Old Testament is thus an evolution, not a revelation; an evolution of the Hebrew mind, and not a revelation from the Divine mind.

Such are the two views of the Old Testament. They are antagonistic in every fibre. In the entire history of opinions, there are no two theories that are more hostile and deadly to each other than these.[1]

---

[1] The antagonism appears in the controversy respecting the Mosaic authorship of the Pentateuch. The Christian Church contends that the legislation of the Pentateuch was supernatural; the entire whole of it being a direct communication from God to Moses, even down to the details of the tabernacle structure (Ex. xxv. 40 ; Num. viii. 4 ; Acts vii. 44 ; Heb. viii. 5). The Rationalists contend that the legislation was natural and non-miraculous, the slow, piece-meal product of the development of the nation. . It required centuries to originate the so-called "codes." "Several generations," says Briggs (Hexateuch, pp. 106, 124), "are necessary to account for such a series of modifications of the same law. There seems to be no room for them in the times of Moses, or Joshua, or Samuel, or David. A priestly code seems to require its historical origin in a dominant priesthood. A prophetic code seems to originate in a period when prophets were in the prominence. A theocratic code suits best a prosperous kingdom, and a period when elders and judges were in authority."

The latter of these two views calls itself the "critical" theory, but the method by which it is attempted to be established is wholly uncritical. Philological criticism, properly so called, is founded upon the text of an author, as this is settled by *manuscripts*, and explained by the rules of grammar and logic. The text itself must be determined by the agreement of manuscripts and the general consensus of editors, and not by individual judgment and caprice. And that interpretation of the text which results from the studies and learning of the great majority of scholars and critics *of all ages* must be regarded as the true one, rather than that which is given by a small minority *of one age.* The catholic interpretation is the most probable interpretation, in sacred as it is in secular philology.

Such is the true critical method universally adopted in profane literature. Should a critic appear in Greek philology, claiming the right to reconstruct the text of the Phædo to such a degree that large portions of it are declared spurious, and this too for the purpose of proving that the doctrine of the immortality of the soul is not taught in it; should he assert that large parts of other dialogues were the product of the time of Alexander, or of the Antonines, and this too for the purpose of showing that Socrates was a materialist and epicurean in philosophy, and agreed with the sophists in opinions generally—should such pseudo-criticism as this be attempted in Greek philology, it would be dismissed with contempt, and declared to be utterly uncritical, because the product of individual preconceptions, in contradiction to historical judgments.

This pseudo-critical method, rarely found in profane literature, has been frequently applied to the sacred writings. While the church universal, patristic, mediæval, and protestant, have been unanimous respecting the authenticity and credibility of both the Old and New Testaments, individuals and schools, from time to time, have denied both. They have been of all grades, deistic, pantheistic, and atheistic; sometimes scoffing, and sometimes serious in tone; but always adopting the same pseudo-critical method, in setting up an individual or a partisan judgment against the catholic. A history of rationalism would show this. But this is impossible here. Our limits confine us to the more recent theories of the so-called "advanced," or "new," or "higher" criticism—for it takes all of these names.

The industry, ingenuity, and perseverance of German scholars have been more successful than those of any others, in attacking the Scriptures of the Old and New Testaments in the rationalistic method. The endeavor was first made to destroy the credibility of the life of Christ and of the doctrines that depend upon it, by assuming the spuriousness of large portions of the four Gospels, and their late origin. All existing manuscripts and all the early testimonies respecting the Gospels and Epistles unquestionably support the traditional opinion respecting their genuineness. Baur and Strauss had no new and different manuscripts to present to scholars, and no new testimony of any force from the first centuries. The only method left to them was conjectural criticism, and a shaping of the text of the Gospels and Epistles to their preconceived idea of Christ, and of the supernatural generally. Their principal reliance was, the assertion of legendary additions to the text, or else of post-apostolic authorship, whenever the exigency required it. The most arbitrary caprice was introduced into New Testament exegesis, by this so-called "critical" method. By it, nearly the entire New Testament becomes a spurious book. Guericke sums up the result of the Tübingen "criticism" in these words: "Matthew, Mark, and Luke are post-apostolic, and more or less legendary; John's gospel arose far down in the second century; the Acts of the Apostles was composed long after the death of Peter and Paul, for the purpose of cloaking over the dissension between these apostles; the Epistle to the Romans is spurious in the last two chapters; Corinthians and Galatians are genuine; but Ephesians, Philippians, Colossians, and Thessalonians are spurious; the Epistles to Timothy, Titus, and Philemon are spurious; the Epistles of Peter, John, James, and Jude are all spurious; the Revelation of John is genuine—by which is meant, that it is a genuine Ebionitish production full of hatred toward Paul and the Pauline Christianity." Such extravagance as this in the treatment of a collection of writings, the text of which has a stronger support in ancient manuscripts than that of Thucydides or Virgil, reminds one of Jortins' remark concerning a critic of this class, that "his craziness consisted in rejecting what all the world received; the opposite folly to which is the receiving what all the world rejects."

A defence of the New Testament appeared in the same country where the attack was made. German learning, industry, and perseverance searched and sifted these postulates and assumptions, and showed their uncritical and unscientific character. The authenticity and credibility of the Gospels now rests upon an argument better worked out in certain directions, and more impregnable to a certain class of objections, than it was previously; because Neander, Ebrard, Tholuck, Bleek, Guericke, Christlieb, and others were led to defend the historical or ecclesiastical view against the rationalistic schools.

The Old Testament is now the point of attack in Germany and Holland, and this attack has affected Great Britain and America to some extent. It is easier to attack the Old Testament than the New, because it has a far greater antiquity. Building upon the view already described, that the religion of Israel is natural and not supernatural, a human literature and not a divine revelation—a view presented with both genius and learning by Ewald—the school of Reuss, Graf, Kuenen, and Wellhausen attempt to prove their points by the same pseudo-critical method, of postulating the spuriousness and late origin of large parts of the Old

Testament, and particularly of the Pentateuch. It is with this that the church just now is concerned, and in regard to which it has a duty to perform, viz., the duty of refuting it.

And here it is important to notice that much depends upon the manner in which the refutation is attempted. No middle view between the historical and the rationalistic can long stand, or will succeed in the end. Middle theories, generally, are failures; being absorbed ultimately by one or the other between which they try to mediate. The history of this Old Testament controversy in Germany is instructive and a warning. In that country, the position of some evangelical defenders of the New Testament was uncertain and wavering, when the Old Testament was in question. Schleiermacher cannot be regarded as positive in maintaining the inspiration of either Testament — certainly not of the Old. But that class of substantially evangelical theologians who were influenced by him, though nearer the creeds of the Reformation than Schleiermacher on all doctrinal points, yet adopted a vacillating view of the Old Testament that weakened them whenever they were called to defend it against attacks. Had this class of theologians taken a more decided attitude, and firmly maintained the traditional view of the Old Testament, as they did of the New; had they contended for the supernatural origin of the Pentateuch, and especially its freedom from mythical elements, as consistently and constantly as Hengstenberg and Hävernick did, the subsequent history of opinion in the German church would have been different. The authenticity of the Old Testament would, to-day, have a recognition in Germany more like that which the New Testament has. The middle theory of partial, instead of plenary, inspiration, which they adopted; the separation of the doctrines of the Old Testament from the historical narratives in which they were imbedded, and the assertion that inspiration attaches to doctrine but not to history, opened the way for a yet looser and more fatal theory. For if the historical account of the exodus, and of the journeyings of the children of Israel, is only ordinary ancient history like the early annals of Egypt and Assyria; if legendary matter, in larger or smaller amount, is mixed with elements of fact in all the Old Testament narratives from Adam to Moses, as it is in all early secular history, then doubt and uncertainty will inevitably pass over to the doctrines and institutions associated with this history. What becomes of the divine authority of the decalogue, if it was not actually given to Moses by the finger of God on the peaks of Sinai; if those thunderings and lightnings, and the sound of a trumpet, and the voice of Jehovah, are either in whole or in part mythical imagination and coloring, and not veritable history? It is impossible successfully to maintain the credibility of the doctrines of the Bible while denying that of the narratives which it contains. Strauss well understood this; and therefore he devoted the energies of as acute and ingenious a mind as ever any special pleader possessed, to prove that the narratives in the four Gospels were not historical but mythical. If he had succeeded in his endeavor to demonstrate that the miraculous birth, the miraculous acts, and especially the miraculous resurrection of Jesus Christ were fictions and not facts, legends and not history, he would have succeeded in overthrowing the Christian religion. If Christ be not risen, human faith in him is vain.

It follows, then, that in the contest between these two theories a half-way method, either of defence or of attack, is useless in the end. The truth may be given away by conceding too much to the opponent in the outset; or taking for granted as a fact what is not such. "Why is it," said a shrewd man to a company of scientific friends, "why is it that a pail of water weighs no more with a fish swimming in it, than when the fish is removed?" Various answers were given. After obtaining their explanations, the questioner asked them if they were certain that the fact was as the question implied. The alleged contradictions in the four Gospels must first be shown to be really there, before an attempt to remove them is made. The alleged variety of wholly diverse codes in the Pentateuch must be established as a fact, before any endeavor is made to harmonize them with each other. And there is all the more reason for this precaution, because of the utter absence of unanimity among the rationalistic critics on this point, and their continual change of schemes. It is a guerrilla warfare on their part. Gesenius, De

Wette, Ewald, and Bleek say that Deuteronomy was composed long after the rest of the Pentateuch. Von Bohlen, Vater, Vatke, and Reuss assert that it was written first, and is the source of the ceremonial parts of Exodus, Leviticus, and Numbers. Some put the Elohist before the Jehovist ; others reverse the order. Ewald finds seven different documents, and five different authors, in the Pentateuch ; others see two different documents, and two different authors.

A most searching criticism, therefore, should be applied first of all to points of this kind, and the question be raised immediately, whether there is any such difficulty as is asserted by the rationalist, and whether a harmony of the Pentateuch is impossible upon the traditional view. For if this impossibility be conceded in the outset without any inquiry or contention ; if these unproved assertions of the rationalist respecting inherent and intrinsic contradictions, and spuriousness or late origin of the text, are granted, it will be impossible to maintain the Mosaic authorship of the Pentateuch. If it be allowed in the start that Deuteronomy, in linguistic particulars and style generally, and especially in regard to the sacerdotal and ritualistic institutions described in it, is so utterly different from the other books of the Pentateuch that it could not have originated in the time of Moses, then it will be necessary to show, if possible, that it may have been composed in the time of Josiah, or later yet. But this is the point first to be settled, and, in settling it the advocate of the traditional view has greatly the advantage. For the more the Pentateuch is studied, the more impossible it is to prove or to believe that it is post-exilic. Saying nothing of its close connection with Egypt, and almost total disconnection with Babylon, such a burdensome religious constitution as that of the Pentateuch could not have been imposed in the time of Ezra upon a nation that previously had known nothing of it. That an agricultural people, after having lived for centuries with no such arrangement, should all at once and suddenly agree to cease from labor one day in every seven, and one whole year in every fifty years; that all of the male population should be willing to go up three times annually to Jerusalem for religious services; that they should go through a round of numerous and expensive sacrifices; and lastly, should contribute one-tenth of their whole income to religion—that a people, not having done this previously, should suddenly make such an entire revolution in their manners and customs, is unheard of, and inexplicable by anything that appears in the condition of the Jewish nation on their return from Babylon. That an enslaved people, not yet a nation, fleeing out of Egypt under the guidance of a leader like Moses supported by the immediate presence of Jehovah in miracles and wonders, should be willing to adopt suddenly, and for the first time, such a burdensome system, is probable enough; but that a people a thousand years old, with no such guide as Moses, and no such supernaturalism as that of the Red Sea and Sinai, should be willing, is incredible.[1]

Consider, also, another particular in which the advocate of the traditional view has greatly the advantage; viz., in respect to the age and genuineness of documents. Contemporaneous opinion respecting the authorship of writings, other things being equal, is more trustworthy than that of any other age; and the older testimony is, the nearer it is to contemporaneous. Whether the Pentateuch was composed by Moses, could be better decided by a learned Jew of the first century with his means of information, than by a learned German of the nineteenth century with his means; for the same reason that the opinion of a learned Greek of the age of Alexander respecting the authenticity of Aristotle's Organon, would weigh more than that of a learned Englishman of this day. The nearer any age is to the origin of writings, the more likely it is to know the actual facts regarding the author.

Upon such a point as authorship, therefore, the later ages, speaking generally, must adopt the views of the earlier, unless discoveries are made which absolutely prove that the traditional view is

[1] The following observation of Coleridge is in point: "One striking proof of the genuineness of the Mosaic books is this—they contain precise prohibitions, by way of predicting the consequences of disobedience, of all those things which David and Solomon actually did, and gloried in doing : raising cavalry, making a treaty with Egypt, laying up treasure, and polygamising. Now, would such prohibitions have been fabricated in those kings' reigns, or afterward ? Impossible."—Table Talk, May 20, 1830.

an error. But such discoveries are very rare. And, certainly, with respect to the authorship of the Pentateuch, or of the Gospels, no such conclusive discovery has been made by a modern. In adopting, therefore, the traditional view of the authorship of the Old Testament, the Biblical critic is taking the same course that scholars in profane literature take. The belief in the genuineness of the Platonic dialogues rests upon a testimony that comes down from a distance of two thousand years. But any critic who should now assert the spuriousness of this collection merely because the testimony is very ancient, and only a few names of individual witnesses can be mentioned, would be called upon to give decisive reasons why the traditional opinion should be surrendered in favor of *his* view. Any critic who should be able to overthrow the established historical opinion respecting the genuineness of the writings commonly ascribed to the principal Greek and Roman authors, and to prove that all preceding classical learning and reasoning have been mistaken, would be a remarkable one. None such has appeared.

CONJECTURAL CRITICISM

There are two views of the origin of the Bible. 1. That it is the production of a limited circle of authors mostly contemporaneous with the events, whose names are mentioned in the work itself, and who were divinely inspired for the purpose of producing a book having infallible accuracy and authority. 2. That it is the production of late and unknown editors, who gathered up oral traditions from unknown and often mythical sources, and put them in the form in which they now appear. The first is the Historical view, or that commonly held in ancient, mediæval, and modern Christendom. The second is the Fragmentary theory, and is confined to individuals and schools in modern Christendom. According to the historical theory, the Pentateuch has Moses for its responsible and inspired author. According to the fragmentary theory, with the exception of a few parts which perhaps may be ascribed to Moses, no man knows who wrote the Pentateuch, any more than where the sepulchre of Moses is. According to the historical theory, the four Gospels are the inspired productions of four men, Matthew, Peter-Mark, Paul-Luke, and John, who received and obeyed their Lord's commission to prepare his biography for the use of the church in all time. According to the fragmentary theory, the four Gospels are the uninspired product of unauthorized persons, later than the apostles, who gathered up the traditions concerning Christ that were floating about in the church, and wrought them into their present shape. Such, briefly stated, is the substantial difference between the two theories. One ascribes the Bible to known and infallible authors; the other to unknown and fallible editors.

1. The first objection to the fragmentary theory of the origin of the Scriptures is that it is late and modern. This, to some persons, is a recommendation. But in estimating theories, if time is to be taken into account, one that has all time behind it is preferable to one that has only a fraction. To be modern and new is a good recommendation for the fashion of a hat, but not for an opinion in science. The latest intelligence from the stock market is more valuable than the latest intelligence in Hebrew. The superficiality characteristic of the present decade is due to a rage for "the last thing out," and the neglect of ancient and standard learning. If a person's reading is confined to works composed in his own time, he will become the victim of a theorist or a coterie of them. His knowledge will be narrow, while he supposes it to be omniscient.

The hypothesis that the Scriptures are a collection and combination by unknown editors is a modern conjecture. Though occasionally broached in the Ancient church, it obtained no currency. It dates from Spinoza and Hobbes, in the seventeenth century, and more particularly in the eighteenth century from Astruc (1725), who applied it to the Pentateuch, and Semler (1750), who applied it to the Gospels and the canon generally. The newness of the theory is an objection to it. For it is highly improbable that all the investigations of Biblical philologists for seventeen hundred years, which corroborate the traditional theory of the origin of the Bible, should suddenly be invalidated by the alleged discoveries of a few theorists in the eighteenth and nineteenth centuries. Sudden conversions in religion, like that of St. Paul, are possible, but they suppose an Almighty Author. Such a sudden revolution in Biblical criticism as the refutation of the historical theory and the demonstration of the fragmentary, would be a phenomenon without parallel in literary history.

2. A second objection to the fragmentary theory is, that it is wholly conjectural. Conjecture has its place in all investigation, but it is a very narrow place. It must be employed cautiously and sparingly, and only by the most learned, balanced and judicial minds. That which now goes under the name of "higher criticism" was formerly known as "conjectural criticism," when those standard editions of the Greek and Roman classics were being prepared by the great scholars of the sixteenth and seventeenth centuries, which

it would now be beyond the power of the nineteenth century to produce, because of its neglect of classical literature and overestimate of physical science. But when these crudite editors of the classics used the conjectural method, it was infrequently and timidly. Whoever ventured to declare a passage to be spurious, or to suggest a new reading that differed from the manuscripts, or new interpretations that departed from those of previous scholars, must furnish strong and conclusive reasons. His *ipse dixit* would not do. Individual opinions when contradictory to historical were looked upon with suspicion, even when there was extraordinary learning and acumen. Bentley was the most learned classical scholar of his century, and was better qualified to make use of conjecture in editing the Greek and Latin classics than any other one of his time ; but Pope, probably with some of the extravagance and injustice of satire, said of his editions of Milton and Horace :

> "To Milton lending sense, and Horace wit,
> He made them write what poet never writ."

But this fear of conjectural criticism, and caution in its use, is not characteristic of those modern schools of Biblical philology which are now employing it for the purpose of recasting the Scriptures, in order to force them into the service of anti-supernaturalism and infidelity. In endeavoring to disprove the Mosaic authorship of the Pentateuch, and the Apostolic authorship of the Gospels, they rely chiefly upon the inventiveness and ingenuity of their own intellects in constructing schemes that are unsupported either by documents or testimony. The utmost rashness and recklessness characterize their work. It would be startling, and a refutation of the whole procedure, to see a Hebrew text of the Pentateuch actually edited and published in accordance with the conjectural criticism of Kuenen and Wellhausen, or a Greek text of the Gospels in accordance with that of Baur and Strauss. Critics of this class make hypothesis the substance and staple of their method, employing it excessively and almost exclusively. The Hebrew text of the Pentateuch, without regard to the manuscripts and the history of the text, and with no support from them, is arbitrarily parcelled out into sections and fractions designated by letters of the alphabet, and this fragment is assigned to the "Elohist," and that to the "Jehovist," this to Moses and that to an unknown editor after the exile, and a fifth to the time of Josiah, purely upon the individual guess of a man living three thousand years after Moses. The Greek text of the four Gospels, without regard to the authority of numerous, and some of them very ancient manuscripts, and in contradiction to the early testimony of scholars like Origen and Jerome, and the consensus of Christendom for fifteen hundred years, is declared to be spurious in all such Gospels, and also in such Epistles, as the scheme of the critic requires.

Such effrontery and dogmatism in claiming that the *ipse dixit* of an individual or a party outweighs the evidence of documents and historical data, and the learning of all the Christian centuries, would not be endured for a moment within the province of secular literature. Nor is such "higher criticism" as this attempted in this department. No one has endeavored to disconnect the Platonic dialogues from the name of Plato, and to prove that they are the production of later editors working over oral discourses of Socrates that were floating in fragmentary form among the circles of the Academy. No one has pretended to a knowledge of Greek literature so much superior to that of the Cudworths and Porsons, the Hermanns and Stallbaums, as to be able to reverse their judgment and demonstrate the spuriousness and late origin of large portions of the Phædo, Symposium, and Laws. No one has composed a new life of Socrates, evincing that the traditional account of him is erroneous. The credulity that trusts such assurance as this is to be found only among students of the Bible. "The children of this world are in their generation wiser than the children of light." The only important attempt of this kind in classical literature, that of Wolf, though made by the most eminent German philologist of the eighteenth century, was a failure. He did not succeed in persuading the classical circles that the Iliad and Odyssey were not the work of Homer, but of a school of rhapsodists whose oral poems were collected and combined by later editors.

3. A third objection to the fragmentary theory

of the origin of the Bible is that it is fatal to its inspiration. If, as a conjectural critic asserts, "the great body of the Old Testament was written by authors whose names are lost in oblivion" (Briggs-Inaugural, p. 33), it was written by uninspired men. Because inspiration, from the nature of the case, was always bestowed upon a particular known person, and is so represented. "God spake unto Moses." "The Lord said unto Samuel." "The word of God came to Nathan." "The word of the Lord came unto David." "The vision of Isaiah which he saw concerning Judah." "The word of the Lord came expressly unto Ezekiel." "God at sundry times spake unto the fathers by the prophets," and the names of these prophets were well known to those to whom they spoke. Inspiration is not an indiscriminate gift of God, like air and water, to anybody and everybody, in any age and every age. It is an extraordinary and rare gift to only a few persons, chosen out of the common mass for the purpose of Divine communications to mankind. The "holy men of God" who "spake as they were moved by the Holy Ghost" were not anonymous authors, like Walter Scott when he was the great Unknown. They belonged to the Jewish people, and their names are generally mentioned in the Bible in connection with the fact of their inspiration and the time of its occurrence. The moment therefore that inspiration is severed from known individuals, the moment it is disconnected from the college of prophets and apostles, it becomes inspiration "in the air," without locality, history, or evidence. The self consistent advocates of the fragmentary theory, like Kuenen and Wellhausen, perceive that it is incompatible with inspiration, and deny inspiration ; but some who are less logical, or more under the restraints of an evangelical connection, try to retain the inspiration of the Pentateuch while denying that Moses is its author. The Pentateuch, they say, was composed long after Moses by some persons no one knows who ; but whoever they were they were inspired. This is the inspiration of imaginary persons like John Doe and Richard Roe, and not of definite historical persons like Moses and David, Matthew and John, chosen of God by name and known to men.

The notion that there is an inspiration outside of the Biblical circle of the prophets and apostles, existing anywhere and at all times, and that the unknown collectors and redactors of the Scriptures partook of it, was invented by the recent latitudinarian party in the Presbyterian church who adopted the critical principles of Rationalism, but who from their ecclesiastical connection did not venture to draw the logical conclusion of all Rationalists and deny inspiration altogether. The assertion that an utterly unknown person was an inspired person is absurd on the face of it, and untenable because it is not only destitute of proof but is absolutely incapable of proof. No *testimony* is possible in the case. No one has ever seen an unknown man work a miracle as evidence of a divine commission; has heard him speak a prophecy or deliver a divine message while under a divine afflatus; or can attest that he was the author of a particular book of Scripture. No proof whatever on such important points as these can be furnished by eye-witnesses and contemporaries. An unknown man, virtually, has no contemporaries; for as no one knows when the man himself lived, so no one knows when his contemporaries did. The only testimony conceivable in the case is that of the conjectural critic, living two or three thousand years later, who merely asserts that the unknown author of the Pentateuch, or Psalms, or Isaiah, was inspired. This, of course, is not of the nature of testimony, because the critic "is of yesterday and knows nothing" of ancient events, and has observed nothing with any of his senses, in the case.

The absurdity of this notion is apparent, when it is considered that nothing whatever can be predicated of an utterly unknown person, any more than of a non-existent one. Attributes and characteristics of every kind are impossible in both cases alike. No one would think of asserting that an utterly unknown man, any more than a non-existent man, is black, or has a large nose, or underwent a surgical operation. Such particulars as these can neither be affirmed nor denied in these instances, because nothing at all is known about the person in question, and consequently nothing can be testified to. But an inspiration that cannot be proved is worthless. Mankind demand evidence when the claim to this unique and extraordinary gift of God to the human mind is made. And in the instance of that limited circle of prophets and apostles whose names are mentioned in Scripture as the authors of most of the books, and are copied from Scripture into the catalogue of the canonical books given in the Westminster Confession (i. 2), and into all the Christian creeds that contain articles upon this point, the proof is forthcoming. That Moses, Samuel, David and Isaiah were inspired, rests upon testimony of two kinds: first, that of Jesus Christ, who authoritatively indorses the inspiration of the traditional authors of the Old Testament; secondly, that of contemporaries and those who were nearest to contemporaries. These latter do not authoritatively indorse like the Son of God, but only give witness respecting the prophetical and apostolical authorship. The evidence in this last instance relates only to canonicity, and is precisely like that for the authorship of the writings of Plato and Cicero, respecting which there is no scepticism in the literary world. The evidence in the first instance is wholly unlike anything in secular literature, and infinitely higher and more trustworthy, provided that Jesus Christ was not an impostor, but God incarnate. The assertion of the critic to whom we have referred, that it is "not of great importance that we should know the names of those authors chosen by God to mediate his revelation" (Briggs-Inaugural, p. 33), overlooks the fact that in revealed religion the credibility of a doctrine depends upon its *source*, as well as upon its nature and contents. For example, the doctrine of the resurrection of the body, judged by its mere contents, is the same in the Egyptian Book of the Dead (Rawlinson's Egypt, I. 319) as in 1 Cor. 15:51, 52. Resurrection is resurrection. But when Egyptian priests assert a resurrection of the body, and St. Paul asserts it, the ground of belief for the doctrine is wholly different in the two instances. And the difference is due to the difference in the authorship. In case of an *ipse dixit* like this, it is important to know who *ipse* is. St. Paul is a known man, and his inspiration can be proved. The Egyptian priests are unknown men, and if they were known there is no proof that they were inspired. Hence the questions of authorship, and genuineness of authorship, have always been regarded in Christian apologetics as vital; and the endeavor from the first has been to connect every one of the books of the Old and New Testaments with some known inspired prophet or apostle. The sceptical criticism, on the contrary, has from the first endeavored to disconnect them. That the first endeavor is difficult in regard to a few of the books, is no reason why the whole position of Christian apologetics should be surrendered, and the authorship of the Bible be ascribed to utterly unknown persons, living no one knows where, and no one knows when.

A deadly thrust is given to the doctrine of infallible inspiration, by the denial that "the Scriptures were written by or under the superintendence of prophets and apostles." (Briggs-Inaugural, p. 32.) This severs them entirely from that particular circle of persons who were called of God by name, and inspired by him to receive and record his supernatural communications. The Westminster Confession, as well as the creeds of Christendom generally, teaches that the Scriptures were composed by or under the superintendence of the prophets of the Old dispensation, and the apostles of the New, and that these persons, and these only, were "the holy men of God who spake as they were moved by the Holy Ghost." One of the principal endeavors of Christian apologetics from Eusebius down, has been to present the proof of this. And there is a general consensus in Christian apologetics, respecting the authorship of the canonical books mentioned in the Westminster Confession (i. 2). Its contention is, that they were composed by the persons to whom from the first they have been ascribed by both Jewish and Christian tradition. Respecting the authorship of a few of these books, there is a difference of opinion among Christian apologetes. But the authorship in these instances is still *kept within the inspired circle of prophets and apostles*, and the endeavor is always made to give the name of the prophet or apostle. It is assumed that if it could be incontrovertibly proved that a particular book was not written by or under the guidance of a prophet or apostle, it is not inspired. Rationalistic criticism dissents from and combats this consensus of Christian apologetics. The reason for this constant aim and office of all the learning of evangelical as opposed to rationalistic criticism is: first, because the books themselves generally claim to be the composition of these particular persons to the exclusion of all other extraneous persons known or unknown; and second, because there were no other inspired persons but the prophets and apostles. If the Bible cannot be proved to be written by the prophets and apostles, it cannot be proved to be inspired at all; because *it cannot be proved that there were ever any human beings whatever, excepting these prophets and apostles, that were "moved by the Holy Ghost."* The origin of an inspired writing must therefore be brought by competent testimony within this inspired circle or nowhere. And if it is thus brought by ancient Jewish testimony in the case of the Old Testament, and by ancient Christian testimony in the case of the New, it cannot be said to be the product of an utterly unknown author even in the instances when the name of the particular prophet or apostle is debated. For this testimony connects it with a *definite circle* of inspired persons whose nationality, time, and place are known. If, for illustration, there is sufficient reason for believing, from Patristic testimony, that the epistle to the Hebrews was composed under the supervision of St. Paul, the doubt whether the penman was Luke, Apollos, or Barnabas, does not make it the product of an "unknown inspired man." The maintenance of this position in apologetics is vital, and has always been so considered. In disconnecting, as the conjectural critic does, the Pentateuch from Moses as its responsible and inspired author, and connecting it with an unknown editor or editors a thousand years later than Moses, he has destroyed its inspiration, because, as we have seen, an unknown man cannot be proved to be one of the "holy men of God who spake as they were moved by the Holy Ghost." There is no testimony or tradition, either for him or against him, in regard to this point. In algebra, the value of the unknown x can be determined, but there is no assignable value to an unknown inspired man. The denial that the Pentateuch is what our Lord frequently called it, "the book of Moses" (Mark 12:26; Luke 24:27; John 7:19, 22, 23), has the same effect upon its inspired authority and credibility, which the denial that the four Gospels were composed by the four Evangelists has upon the inspiration and credibility of the only source the world has for the life of its divine Redeemer. There were no infallibly inspired persons upon earth between A.D. 33 and A.D. 100, excepting the company of the Apostles chosen by Christ to be the founders of his church, and, if we may so say, his literary executors to write his life for the church in all time; and if the four Gospels were not composed by them, or under their superintendence, they are neither inspired nor infallible. No persons but these were authorized or qualified to prepare the memoirs of his marvellous origin and generation, and of his merciful and sorrowful life (Luke 24:49; John 14:26; 15:26; Acts 1:8).

Whoever denies this, and enlarges the circle of New Testament inspiration by asserting that others than the Apostles were inspired by the Holy Ghost, is bound to prove his assertion. As the four Evangelists do in the instance of the "Twelve Apostles," he must mention the names of the persons, the circumstances under which they were called to this office, and the supernatural signs of their inspiration (Matt. 10:1–5; Mark 3:14–19; Luke 6:13–16). The burden of proof is upon the affirmative, not upon the negative. The inspiration of a Biblical writing, therefore, stands or falls with its authenticity and genuineness. If its authorship is forged and spurious; if it is falsely ascribed to the prophets and apostles, and is not their work; it was not written by "holy men of God who spake as they were moved by the Holy Ghost."

PSEUDO-HIGHER CRITICISM

Higher criticism is a legitimate branch of human science. There is nothing in the mere name that should awaken fear or suspicion. It is an instrument which when rightly employed establishes truth, not error; and has been so employed in both secular and sacred philology from the beginning. It is only the misemployment of it that is to be dreaded. As there is a true and false philosophy, theology, physics, and æsthetics, so there is a true and a false higher criticism.

Higher criticism is that discipline which endeavors to determine the text of an author from *internal* considerations; such as the connexion of thought, the agreement or disagreement between themselves of the truths and facts presented, the harmony of customs and institutions with the environment in which they are said to have existed, and other like data for forming an opinion respecting the original writing. Lower criticism, on the other hand, endeavors to determine the text of an author from *external* considerations; principally by examining the extant manuscripts and early versions, and by a comparison deducing the most probable text. It is plain that there is greater liability to the abuse of the higher criticism than of the lower, because in the former more depends upon individual opinion and conjecture. When two scholars look at the Vatican and Sinaitic manuscripts for the Greek text of the New Testament actually written in them, there is little room for a difference of view as to what it is. But when two scholars read the Hebrew Deuteronomy in order to decide whether there are contradictions in it, or such a diversity in language as to imply several authors, there is large opportunity for difference of opinion. It is for this reason, that the higher criticism needs the restraint and guidance of the lower. Those conjectural critics who attempt to determine the original text wholly by internal considerations, without taking into view the testimony of manuscripts, versions, and the history of the text, are almost certain to commit errors. There is nothing of an objective nature to check their subjective prejudices, or fancies, or wishes. This last remark is the key to the wholly different conclusions to which the genuine and the spurious higher criticism have respectively arrived. Critics like Hengstenberg, Hävernick, Delitzsch, Neander, and Tholuck in Germany; like Lowth, Lardner, Graves, Macdonald, and Lightfoot in Great Britain; by the use of the higher criticism *combined* with the lower, have agreed with the learning of Christendom for two millenniums in affirming the authenticity of the Old and New Testaments; while critics like Semler, Eichorn, Strauss, and Wellhausen on the continent; like Geddes, Robertson Smith, and Driver in Great Britain; by the use of the higher criticism *severed* from the lower, have asserted the spuriousness of large portions of the Word of God.[1] Their method consists in assuming without proof the truth of a mere hypothesis of their own and then working under it.

In our young days, we listened to a lecture upon ancient Babylon by a person who knew nothing about criticism high or low, but who unconsciously adopted the method now in vogue among that class of specialists who claim to have the latest intelligence in Biblical Criticism, and to have made discoveries in the Bible that have escaped the notice of all the learning of Christendom until recently. Our lecturer illustrated his description of the walls, towers, and gates of the city, by a set of rudely drawn and colored pictures. At one point in his discourse, he made a statement which drew somewhat upon the credulity of his audience, that the brass gates of the city were two hundred feet in height, adding, however, that some historians judged them to be only fifty feet high. "But," said he, "this is an error, for you see it is not so in the *picture*." We have often been reminded of this mode of reasoning, by the method of the pseudo-higher critics. They first invent a scheme respecting the origin of the Bible, and

[1] "The age and authorship of the books of the Old Testament" (says Driver, Introduction, p. xxxi.) "can be determined only on the basis of the internal evidence; no external evidence worthy of credit exists."

then shape all their studies and publications by it. The received text of the Pentateuch, as it exists in all the Hebrew manuscripts, is analyzed and labelled in accordance with their preconceived theory that the Pentateuch is not the production of a single known author, but of many unknown authors. This theory corresponds to the picture of our lecturer. Anything that agrees with it is correct, anything that disagrees is incorrect. The critic begins with assuming that the traditional text is composite. He does not attempt to prove that it is the work of a variety of authors by the only method that can prove it, and by the method invariably adopted by really learned critics in determining the origin of the text of any classical writer—namely, by the comparison of manuscripts, versions, and contemporary or early testimony.[1] Critics like Kuenen, Wellhausen, and Driver do none of this scientific work in support of their fundamental position; and for the good reason that they cannot. Such a conclusive argument as this, would require manuscripts of the Pentateuch differing from the traditional, and actually containing such varieties in structure, diction, and sentiment as would necessarily infer different au-

[1] A writer in the Edinburgh Review for July, 1892, after a specification of some scores of palpable falsifications of the statements of the Pentateuch, made by Wellhausen for the purpose of evincing discrepancies and interpolations in it, remarks "that 'interpolations' can be established, if at all, only by the evidence of manuscripts and versions, and cannot be allowed merely on the ground of the critic's authority." This article incontrovertibly demonstrates the untrustworthy scholarship of the present leader of the Pseudo-Higher Criticism.

thors. But no such manuscripts have ever been heard of. So far as such diplomatic proof is concerned, there is no more evidence that the Pentateuch was composed by a series of authors covering a thousand years or more of time, than there is that the writings of Plato and Aristotle were. And the reason why this imaginative conjectural method has not been employed in classical philology, and the text of Plato and Aristotle has not been hacked and hewed by it, is that real learning and sound judgment have held undisputed sway in this province, while sacred philology for moral and theological reasons has been invaded from time to time by schemers and sciolists.

As there is none of this historical objective proof of the composite origin of the Pentateuch, the critic of this class flees to a subjective method. He takes the only text there is and manufactures a variety into it. He decides by a volition that this passage came from an unknown document which he calls J, and that from another which he designates by E, and a third from another noted by P, and a fourth from still another distinguished by D, and affirms all this with an assurance that is in inverse proportion to any actual demonstrated knowledge in the case. In this way he spins the scheme of the Elohist and the Jehovist, the Priest and the Deuteronomist, out of his own head, and contorts the Hebrew text up to it. Some one has taken the trouble to count up the number of these cobwebs, and finds that already there are six hundred and three upon the Old Testament and one hundred and forty-four on the New. In this process the clauses, verses, and paragraphs of the Pentateuch are almost microscopically divided. There is an utter solution of continuity. Parts which to both the learned and the common mind seem naturally and vitally connected, are torn asunder, alive and bleeding. The connection, beauty, and symmetry of the composition are wholly destroyed. The printed page upon which the results are expressed, like that of Driver's Introduction to the Old Testament, has more the look of a treatise in algebra than of ordinary English composition. There is a multitude of little sentences notated with small letters and figures similar to the notation of squares and cubes in mathematics, making the attempt to read the page much like that of picking up pins. When the new Hebrew lexicon that is to be adjusted to this scheme is published, the process of committing words to memory will be drier than ever.

But the claim is made by the advocates of this view of the Pentateuch that all the learning of "the day" is with them. Even if this were true, it would be necessary, in order to establish their superiority, to prove that all the learning of "the day" is greater than all the learning of all the past generations of scholars, and that Biblical study has yielded more solid results in the last fifty years than in the preceding eighteen hundred and fifty. But it is not true that all the learning of the last fifty years is on the side of the conjectural criticism, and the composite authorship of the Pentateuch. The test of the prevalence and power of a theory, is the amount and kind of literature produced by it. How much of the Biblical commentary, sermons, ethics, apologetics and theology of the last fifty years rests upon the pseudo-higher criticism as its base? Only a tittle of it. The influence that is now radiating through Christendom from these departments, is overwhelmingly that of the old historical criticism. It is true that the new theory just now is exerting a little more than the average influence of error, but only because, owing to the apathy and toleration of the evangelical churches, it has worked its way somewhat into their membership, and through this prestige has obtained a circulation it never could have got by its own power of locomotion; as a barnacle when it has attached itself to a man-of-war is able to circumnavigate the globe. Take only a single department for illustration. Within the last thirty years, two commentaries upon the whole Bible have been published and widely circulated in America and Great Britain: Lange's and the Speaker's. The former contains the best results of the conservative German criticism, worked over and made still more conservative by American and English scholars. The latter is the work of the ripest scholarship of the English Episcopal Church. What commentary upon the whole Bible, having extensive circulation, has been produced by the opposing criticism, during this day of vaunted improvement and new discovery in Biblical exegesis? A few scattered commentaries upon single books of Scripture have been composed in the interest of the new criticism, but they are only one to hundreds of the like produced by thorough students of the historical class. The erudite commentary of Keil and Delitzsch has had the widest circulation in Great Britain and America of any unrevised and purely German one, and this proceeds generally upon the traditional theory of the origin and authorship of the Scriptures. The learned and able special treatises upon the Pentateuch of Hengstenberg and Hävernick, of Graves and Macdonald, are standard and classical; and no works produced by the specialists of the new criticism are comparable to them, in respect to that union of learning with judgment, which is indispensable to sound interpretation. For in order to be a thorough and accurate interpreter of an inspired book like the Bible, something in addition to a lexical and grammatical knowledge of Hebrew is required. If this were all, a Jewish Rabbi, with his vernacular knowledge of the Jewish Scriptures, and of the immense mass of Rabbinical literature, would be superior to all Christian exegetes. It was said of one of the first of English jurists, that all his legal learning passed into his judgment before he used it. In these days of revived study of the Hebrew and its cognates, it would be well to remember that philological learning must be combined with tact, insight, power to trace the connection of thought, a reference to the analogy of doctrine, and spiritual sympathy with spiritual ideas and truths, in order to a profound and accurate interpretation of the Word of God.

Thirty years ago, one of the most genuine scholars and acutest minds that America has produced, the late Henry B. Smith, gave his estimate of the learning and strength of the rationalistic criticism in a review of what he called "The New Latitudinarianism of England," contained in the "Essays and Reviews," written by members of the English church. Though differing in some secondary particulars, these essayists aimed at the very same revolution in Biblical criticism and dogmatic theology which is now aimed at by the "higher critics" in Great Britain and America. The language of Dr. Smith is as follows: "Most of the writers [of these Essays] have apparently derived their objections and their learning from German sources, and show the danger of beginning such studies without passing through them. The men who are now [1861] leading the theological and philosophical investigations of Germany, are men who have passed through profounder difficulties and more thorough criticism than these Oxford essayists seem to have yet suspected; they have weighed the difficulties with boldness and freedom, and have come out, in spite of them, into the clear light of revealed truth. But all this class of men, the best and brightest lights of Germany, are not known or studied by the Oxford reviewers. That Delitzsch, Keil, Kurtz, Hävernick, Berthau, and Hengstenberg have gone over all their Old Testament difficulties; that Olshausen,

Ebrard, Tholuck, Lange, Stier, and even DeWette, Meyer, and Lücke have replied to many of their New Testament criticisms, they do not seem to have suspected. The essay of Dr. Rowland Williams is simply a résumé of the results of the idealizing school of modern criticism as to the history and doctrines of the inspiration and authority of the Scriptures. No proof is attempted. He seems to think that the whole matter is decided. Where he is not willing to make direct assertions, he throws out wanton insinuations. The tone of self-conscious superiority affected in this essay is not supported by anything contained in it. The Pentateuch is declared to be a gradual growth 'from a Bible before the Bible;' it came into its present form about one thousand or seven hundred years before Christ. That previous documents may have been used in its composition might be conceded, without denying its Mosaic authorship; but Dr. Williams reasons upon it as if Kurtz, and Hengstenberg, and Keil had never written on the question, or noticed all the arguments by which its genuineness has been assailed. He abandons the prophecies of Daniel, transforming them into mere history or conjecture, without condescending to refer to the replies of Auberlen and Hävernick. In fact he gives up all prophecy excepting 'perhaps one passage in Zechariah, one in Isaiah, and one in Deuteronomy on the fall of Jerusalem; though even these few cases tend to melt, if they are not already melted, in the crucible of free inquiry.' Even the Messianic interpretation of the fifty-third of Isaiah is rejected, although for seventeen centuries only two interpreters (excepting Jews) and both of these professed unbelievers, gave it such a non-Messianic sense. Bunsen makes it refer to Jeremiah, or rather to the 'collective Israel.' This last interpretation, as Hengstenberg has unanswerably shown, is most violent, has no analogy in the Old Testament, and demands the most unnatural personifications, as when it is said : 'He made his grave with the rich in his death.'" Smith, "Faith and Philosophy," pp. 177, 178 ; 186–188. This opinion of a distinguished Presbyterian theologian is worthy of the consideration of the present school of Pseudo-Higher Critics in the Northern Presbyterian Church.

FLUCTUATIONS IN GERMAN THEOLOGY

One argument for the late origin and fallibility of the Bible, urged in the present trial for heresy in the Presbyterian church by the accused and his adherents, is the fact that a large number of the professors in German universities are now adopting and defending this view. This is not an argument that has intrinsic weight, because it does not appeal to man's reason and judgment, but to his proneness to follow a fashion. It is like the shopkeeper's reason for buying a particular article: because everybody else is doing so. And it comes in collision with the divine command: "Thou shalt not follow a multitude to do evil."

The influence of Germany upon theology has not been uniform. Sometimes it has been beneficial, and sometimes exceedingly injurious. Orthodoxy and heterodoxy have oscillated in this country more than in any other. Just now, heterodoxy is in the ascendant in the universities, though perhaps not in the churches. It is undoubtedly a fact, and a mournful one, to all who believe that the traditional creeds of Christendom are a correct statement of the contents of Scripture, and that the religious experience founded upon them is the only true experience, that a lapse from these creeds and this faith is now widespread in the country of the Reformation. Such lapses have been frequent there, owing partly to the connection between church and state, and especially to the appointment and supervision of theological teachers by the secular authorities instead of by the living churches themselves. When Tholuck took the chair of Oriental Literature at Halle in 1824, the rationalism of Wegscheider and Gesenius had exclusive sway. Within thirty years he saw its decline and the restoration of evangelical views. But now, if he were alive, he might see again in 1893 much that is like what he saw in 1824. And yet, judging from the past fluctuations of opinion characteristic of the German intellect, it may be hoped that the present apostasy from the œcumenical creeds will again be followed by a reaction and return to the historical Christianity. But in the meantime error is making rapid progress in Germany, and the fact is proposed by the "progressive" party in the evangelical churches of Great Britain and America as an example for imitation. Whoever now adopts a scheme because it is prevalent in the German universities, runs the hazard of adopting a false one.

We have been led to this line of remark by a new phase of heterodoxy which is now becoming influential in Germany. Errors grow in clusters, and lax views concerning the origin and infallibility of the Bible are organically connected with lax views in Christian theology generally. A Leipsic periodical contains an article on "The Present Creed Controversy in Germany" which describes the new movement. "Not for decades," says the writer, "has the Protestant Church passed through such an excitement as that under which she has been laboring for the past months, and which is agitating her yet, from one end of the country to the other." It began with the declaration of two pastors, Schrempf and Längen, that they would no longer use the Apostles' creed in the services of the church, as they could not adopt some of its statements. Their views immediately attracted attention. "Professor Harnack," continues the writer, "being asked by his students whether they should enter upon a movement looking to a removal of the Apostles' creed from the vow of ordination, replied that this should not be done by the students, but added that this venerable creed contained not a few statements at which a historically and dogmatically trained Christian must take offence, especially the statement: 'Conceived by the Holy Ghost, born of the Virgin Mary.'" This repudiation of one of the principal articles of the oldest and most widely accepted of all the Christian creeds by the most popular professor of church history in Germany, and who is influencing English and American students at Berlin, probably, more than any other teacher, excited much interest, and finally "led to a convention at Eisenach of representatives of the more liberal section of the Evangelical church, among whom were fifteen theological professors from the universities of Berlin, Bonn, Breslau, Giessen, Göttingen, Halle, Heidelberg, Jena, Leipsic, Marburg, Tübingen, and ten pastors and high church officials from Prussia, Saxony, Würtemburg, Hesse, and Gotha. This convention made a declaration in which the standpoint of Harnack is endorsed, and pronounced against the immemorial claim of Christendom that the birth of Christ from a virgin is a fundamental article of the Christian faith, the basis of evangelical Christianity, since this birth is mentioned only in the introduction of the two Gospels of Matthew and Luke and is not referred to again in the New Testament." Such is the account of this movement in the Leipsic article.

Here is a body of German theologians and pastors of the highest ecclesiastical position and influence, who deny that Jesus Christ was miraculously conceived by the Holy Ghost and born of a virgin, and in contradiction to all dogmatic history and dogmatic theology declare that this is not one of the essential doctrines of the Christian religion because only *two* of the four Gospels expressly and verbally teach it ! The same argument which some theologians in the Presbyterian church are urging in support of their denial of the infallibility of the Bible as it came from inspired prophets and apostles, namely its present rejection in the German universities, should lead them also to repudiate the doctrine of the incarnation as it is enunciated in the oldest and most generally accepted of the ancient creeds—a creed, moreover, which many of these theologians desire to substitute in place of all the subsequent creeds which define the truths of Scripture more precisely and rigidly.

The sudden emerging into notice of this heresy at this time is instructive, and a warning to all evangelical churches how they wink at and tolerate printed and published error. It is sure to sprout. Some fifty years ago Schleiermacher published in his *Glaubenslehre* (§ 97) his opinion that "Christ had an earthly father, but that by a supernatural operation on the embryo it was cleansed from original sin." This was the denial of his birth from a virgin, yet coupled with the affirmation of his sinlessness. Schleiermacher's hypothesis has lain *perdu* in his theological system until now, attracting little or no attention. Now it comes to the surface, and becomes the nucleus of a large party in the German church. For whether the Eisenach convention are as orthodox as Schleiermacher in holding to the sinlessness of Christ is uncertain; but that they are as heterodox as he is in denying the virginal birth, is clear. A reference to the text of Schleiermacher gives reason for believing that the Eisenach theologians went to him both for their opinion and their reason for it; for they assign the same reason, and make the same Scripture citations.[1]

---

[1] Harnack has recently published his own account of the history of the Apostles' creed, which has been translated and published

It is time for the Presbyterian church, which still has an unrevised Calvinistic creed, and professes to believe that the Scriptures when accurately expounded will yield this creed, to cease taking lessons in theology from German theologians while they are in their present fermentation and unsettled condition. In ordinary circumstances of good health and freedom from contagious disease, nations do not quarantine each other. But when cholera or typhus prevails among a people, it is not regarded as harsh or unfriendly in another people that is particularly exposed to abridge intercourse. England and America, in times past, have received theological benefits from the land of Luther which they acknowledge gratefully. But an indiscriminate adoption of the varieties of progressive and anti-traditional theology now rampant there, would nullify much of the good that has been received in the past. England and America can do more for Germany in her present distracted condition, than Germany can do for them. Provincialism is one

in the *Nineteenth Century* for July, 1893. In this he asserts that "one of the best established results of history is, that the clause, 'Conceived by the Holy Ghost and born of the Virgin Mary' does not belong to the earliest Gospel preaching," and the proof which he gives for this assertion is the further assertion that the Gospels of Matthew and Luke "do not represent the earliest stage of evangelical history." In this affirmation, he is contradicted by the fact that the miraculous conception of Christ by the Holy Spirit is distinctly taught in such very early creeds as that of Irenæus (Adv. Hær. i. 10); of Tertullian (De Virginibus Velandis, c. 1, De Præscrip. c. 13, Adv. Prax. c. 2); and of Origen (Prœm. op περὶ ἀρχῶν, interprete Rufino). See Pearson : Creed, Appendix.

great defect in German learning and authorship. Germans read and quote Germans too exclusively. If German scholars had been for the last century as enterprising and adventurous as English and American scholars have been, and German theology had been as much pervaded by the massive learning, close reasoning, wise judgment, and sound faith of the great lights of English and American theology of the last three centuries, as English and American theology has been by the writings of the German divines of this century, it would have been less marked by eccentricity and departures from historical Christianity ; broader as well as deeper in its structure, because more closely connected with the traditional faith which has been the spinal column of Christendom from first to last ; and less deluded by the phosphoric lights of schemers and schemes. Germany has produced no works superior in first-hand learning, drawn from the original sources and not from encyclopædias and manuals, to the researches of Hooker, Cudworth, Usher, Stillingfleet, Pearson, Bull, and Waterland, and no dogmatic treatises equal in depth and spirituality to those of Howe, Owen, Baxter, Bates, Butler, and Edwards. Yet this large and solid body of theology is almost unknown to the majority of German rationalists.

The English and American churches should remember, also, that the reputation of the numerous theories in Biblical criticism and dogmatic theology that are continually rising and disappearing in Germany is exaggerated and deceptive. It is local, not œcumenical. The so-called "schools" are limited circles connected with a particular university, and composed of professors and "privatdocenten" ambitious to originate a new theory. Their reading lies mainly within the present century, and their citation also. Their effort is to bring their book "up to date," and to examine "the last thing out." In this way, the solid and accurate learning of the great past, and of other countries than their own, becomes neglected, and is contemptuously called "antiquated." The result of this method of authorship, in a country where printing is cheap, is an immense issue of inferior works, of which not one in a thousand becomes a classic in the department to which it belongs. But the number of these publications being "legion," a sort of public opinion is manufactured for the novel and anti-historical hypotheses broached in them, by counting rather than by weighing them, and the arithmetical argument takes the place of the argument from intrinsic truth and reason.

HUMAN ALTERATIONS OF THE FOURTH COMMANDMENT

The importance of a true theory in order to good practice is illustrated by the controversy now going on respecting the observance of the Sabbath. Those who advocate the secularization of the Lord's day take the view that the seventh day of the week was set apart by God merely that man might rest from bodily toil. They defend the Sabbath chiefly upon the ground that the aching muscle, and the tired brain, are better prepared for six days' work by a cessation from physical and mental strain. This theory is part and parcel of that materialism which is undermining American society and institutions. It supposes that the body is of more consequence than the soul, and that the interests of time are superior to those of eternity. According to this view, if it could be shown that man would not be better off physically by six days' toil and one day's rest, the Sabbath would have no claim upon his observance.

The theory of the Sabbath presented in the

Scriptures is directly opposite to this. According to both Moses and Christ, the end for which the seventh day is set apart is *worship*. The purpose is to afford toiling man an opportunity to think of his Maker, and draw nigh to him by prayer and praise. " Six days shalt thou labor and do all thy work, but the seventh day is the Sabbath of the Lord thy God." The descriptions in the Old Testament imply not merely a cessation from manual labor, but from all mental labor that is secular and relates only to earth and time. A divine blessing is promised to him, and to him alone, who turns away his foot " from doing his pleasure on God's holy day, and calls the Sabbath a delight, the holy of the Lord, honorable, and honors him, not doing his own ways, nor finding his own pleasure, nor speaking his own words." Is. 58:13. When Christ denominated himself the Lord of the Sabbath, he meant the Sabbath as thus appointed and described in the Old Testament, and thereby set the seal of his approbation and authority upon it. Accordingly, all the physical and temporal purposes and benefits of the Sabbath must be set second to these religious and spiritual purposes and benefits. When they come—as they do in the train, and as the inevitable consequences of a right observance of the fourth commandment —they are not to be regarded as the chief end of its institution, or the main reason why it was given. An old divine says that merely to abstain from labor without engaging in public worship, is to keep the Sabbath as the cattle keep it.

The truth is that there is nothing *obligatory* in the observance of the Sabbath, unless it be a day of worship. It is a man's solemn duty to worship his Maker, and if he fails to perform it he is guilty, and will be sentenced as such in the great day. When, therefore, you bid him to keep the Sabbath for this purpose, you have a hold upon his conscience, and he cannot combat you except by taking infidel ground, and denying all obligation of this kind. But when you are silent upon this religious point, and tell him to rest on the seventh day because his bodily health requires it, or his mental relaxation makes it necessary, you are presenting merely a prudential and worldly motive, which has no moral force. He can say to you: "I am a better judge in respect to what my own worldly interests require than you are. I think that they will be best promoted by laboring as much as I please, and doing what I like on any and every day of the week."

But it is objected that multitudes will not go to the house of God and worship him on the Sabbath, and therefore it is better to say to them: "Do the next best thing: go into the reading-room and read what you like; go into the park, or out into the country, and breathe the fresh air." This has actually been said by professed ministers of Christ, and, judging from the apathy of many professed followers of Christ, meets approval from a portion of the visible church. This is certainly a bold and reckless dealing with the law of God. Suppose that this method should be adopted with all the commandments, instead of with one of them. Suppose that the minister of the gospel should say to his auditors: "Many of you find it impossible to love God with all your heart; do the next best thing: love your wife and children. Many of you find it difficult to love your neighbor as yourself; do the next best thing: love your farm and your merchandise." What would be thought of that spiritual adviser who should endeavor to persuade a licentious person to take up with fornication in lieu of adultery, and then should crown his labors for the spiritual good of his fellow-creature by assuring him that this will pass for obedience to the seventh commandment?

The duty of the Church, in the present period of attack upon the Lord's day, is plain. It is simply and firmly to teach the teaching that God has given. The Christian ministry must affirm that nothing short of devout and reverential worship of God in the sanctuary, is obedience of the fourth commandment. This, it is true, will convict the great majority of men of sin before the Searcher of hearts. But so does the proclamation of every other one of the ten commandments. Men do not keep the law; but this is no reason for modifying or altering it. The actual and veritable command must be presented, whether men put it in practice or not. The only hope of bringing about correct conduct is in laying down the Divine rule of such conduct. If the rule itself be changed, and evil is put for good, and bitter for sweet, nothing but the most lawless and licentious conduct will result.

The theory recently broached that the reading of newspapers and magazines, riding or sauntering in the country, and similiar occupations and amusements, is what God intended when he said on Mount Sinai, "Remember the Sabbath-day to keep it holy," will prove, in its effects upon society, to be the teaching of a false prophet, and be as destructive as a wolf in sheep's clothing.

LIBERAL BIGOTRY

Dr. Johnson, during his tour to the Hebrides, met with a person who like many in the present day was vehemently opposed to creeds and confessions of faith. His principal objection to them was that they are inconsistent with mental freedom. The human mind, he said, is confined by them, and they ought not to be imposed upon it. To this the hard head and robust commonsense of Johnson made answer, that what the objector called imposition is only a voluntary declaration of agreement in certain articles of faith which a church has a right to require, just as any other society can insist upon certain rules being observed by its members. Nobody is compelled to belong to the church, as nobody is compelled to enter a society. This, however, did not satisfy the pertinacious opponent of creeds; and he continued his objections in the same general strain as before. Johnson then silenced him with the remark: " Sir, you are a bigot to laxness."

Bigotry is a blind and unreasonable devotion to an opinion. It may be found in the ranks of infidelity as frequently as in those of politics or religion. The political and especially the theological bigot has had a full share of attention and criticism. The latitudinarian bigot is a species that has been somewhat overlooked, and taking the text we have quoted from Dr. Johnson, we propose to preach a short sermon upon the subject of Liberal Bigotry.

Our first remark is, that the liberal thinker, as he styles himself, is a bigot in finding fault with a religious denomination to which he does not belong, for making an honest and manly statement of what it believes. The zeal with which he attacks a society with which he is not identified, because it holds certain tenets as the condition of membership, is certainly both blind and unreasonable. By what right does he complain of a body of his fellow-men because, in the exercise of their own judgment, they have come to the conclusion that the creed of Calvin or the creed of Arminius is the truth, and that the doctrine of Socinus or of Swedenborg is error? What reason is there in demanding of a large society that they surrender their convictions respecting such subjects as the trinity, the incarnation, the apostasy, and the redemption, and take in lieu of them the opinions of an individual who styles himself a liberal thinker? There might be some reason in this objecting to distinct statements of religious truth, if the objector were himself concerned in the origin and formation of the society adopting them. If it were still an open question, and the disputant were entitled to a voice, then his zeal against creeds would not necessarily be bigoted. But the churches are already in existence. Neither the latitudinarian nor the downright sceptic had anything to do with their origin or constitution, and they have no more part or lot in them than an American democrat has in the monarchy of England. It is the height of bigotry, therefore, when the unbeliever represents the terms of communion which religious denominations have established not for *him*, but for themselves, as being bigoted and intolerant.

Our second remark is, that the bigot to laxness is himself an inquisitor, and a foe to freely-formed opinion. He is uneasy upon seeing that others have fixed and settled views, and attempts to unsettle them by attacks upon all definite statements of doctrine. Why is he not content with the liberty which he himself enjoys of adopting no particular sentiments, and of maintaining, like the ancient sophists, that there is no absolute truth, and that one thing is just as valid as another? He is allowed his own dislike and rejection of a creed, why should he disallow another man's liking for and adoption of a creed? His complaint over the freely-formed conviction of his fellow-men that the evangelical system is the truth of God, is in reality a protest against their right of private judgment, and a demand that they adopt his opinions upon this point. But this is bigotry. If he would be content with his criticism and attack upon a particular creed, no fault would be found with him. But when, after the criticism and attack, he pronounces the advocate of the creed to be a bigot because he still remains unconvinced by his reasonings and still retains his belief, he passes the line of free and fair discussion, and enters the province of intolerance and bigotry. He does not meet with this treatment from the defender of the faith once delivered to the saints. The charge of bigotry is not often made by the orthodox against the heterodox, but always by the heterodox against the orthodox. Perhaps we are the first since Dr. Johnson to direct attention to the bigotry of laxness. And we do not charge bigotry upon the latitudinarian merely because he attacks the evangelical creed, but because he calls those bigots who are not converted by his arguments.

It is curious to notice how extremes meet. The latitudinarian will be found to be narrow, when he comes to be examined; and the dogmatist will be found to be liberal, when his real position is seen. The former is restless and uneasy upon discovering that his fellow-men in large masses are holding fixed opinions, and are ready to live and die by them. He complains and quarrels with them for so doing. The latter is calm and self-possessed, being satisfied with his freely-formed convictions and his self-consistent creed, and while he does his best to convert to his own views those whom he regards as being in error, yet if he finds himself to be unsuccessful, he enters no querulous complaint and indulges in no bitter intolerance, because he commits all judgment to God and the final day.

The gentle and fair-minded Addison, in one of the *Spectators* (No. 185), directs attention to what he denominates infidel bigotry. "After having treated of these false zealots in religion, I cannot," he says, "forbear mentioning a monstrous species of men who one would not think had any existence in nature, were they not to be met with in ordinary conversation. I mean the zealots in atheism. Infidelity is propagated with as much fierceness and contention, wrath and indignation, as if the safety of mankind depended upon it. There is something so ridiculous and perverse in this kind of zealots, that one does not know how to set them out in their proper colors. They are a sort of gamesters who are eternally upon the fret, though they play for nothing. They are perpetually teasing their friends to come over to them, though at the same time they allow that neither of them shall get anything by the bargain. In short, the zeal of spreading atheism is, if possible, more absurd than atheism itself. I would fain ask one of these bigoted infidels : Supposing all the great points of atheism, such as the casual or eternal formation of the world, the materiality of a thinking substance, the mortality of the soul, the fortuitous organization of the body, the motions and gravitation of matter, and the like particulars, were laid together and formed into a kind of creed, according to the opinions of the most celebrated atheists, I ask, supposing such a creed as this were formed, and imposed upon any one people in the world, whether it would not require an infinitely greater measure of faith, than any set of articles which they so violently oppose. Let me therefore advise this generation of wranglers, for their own and for the public good, to act at least so consistently with themselves, as not to burn with zeal for irreligion, and with bigotry for nonsense."

The present attack upon the Calvinistic creed by the so-called " liberal " and " progressive " parties in Protestantism, is an example of the zeal of bigotry. The particular opponents of Calvinism of whom we are now speaking are not atheists. They are believers in a deity and the principles of morality, and some of them accept a vague form of evangelical doctrine. But the language of Johnson and Addison nevertheless applies to them. In respect to the five points of Calvinism, and the general type of doctrine contained in the Westminster standards, they are bigoted partisans. The zeal which they exhibit in opposition to this intellectual and powerful theology, is as unintelligent and passionate as anything to be found in any annals whatever. And what is worse, it is an unscrupulous zeal not seen among the orthodox. When did the orthodox ever stoop to the method of the " liberal " theologian ? When did Calvinists ever attempt to sap and destroy " progressive " theology, by the plan recommended by some " progressive " theologians for sapping and destroying the Calvinistic faith : the plan of remaining in a denomination after changing one's belief, and trying to subvert the creed of the denomination ? What Calvinists ever advised Calvinists publicly to subscribe an anti-Calvinistic creed, and then teach and defend Calvinism within an anti-Calvinistic denomination? What Calvinist ever advised Calvinists to hold office and take emoluments on anti-Calvinistic foundations? What orthodox body has ever put to its own use endowments that were given for the spread of "progressive" theology ? The history of religious endowments shows without an exception, if we are not mistaken, that it is the looser creed that filches from the stricter, not the stricter from the looser.

Whatever else may be laid to the charge of the advocates of orthodoxy, covert movements, concealed opinions, and double dealing cannot be. They have never burrowed under ground; and they have never pretended to be what they are not. And they have insisted that all who join them shall do so in good faith, and hold a common creed. For this they are charged with narrowness and bigotry ! The charge falls upon the other party.

"ORTHODOX DISBELIEF"

A RECENT number of a religious journal contained an article upon endless suffering by one who calls himself an "Orthodox Disbeliever" which is deserving of some remark, because it probably expresses the sentiments of a certain class which though not large may be increasing. The writer describes himself as expecting to enter the orthodox ministry, and as having begun a theological course. He found "to his surprise" that he was not orthodox on the subject of endless punishment. "With sorrow I turned aside," he says, "from the ministry, to the great regret of many friends, few of whom knew the reason. I feared I could not safely and honestly pass the ordeal of an examining council. If my disbelief had begun two or three years later, I should probably have been in the ministry, and should now be preaching future punishment [not *endless* punishment] without emphasis of details, the more earnestly on account of the severe mental conflict. I retain my standing in an orthodox church, keeping my views to myself."

This is a frank confession of a want of frankness. Had this "Orthodox Disbeliever" openly said to his friends, "I cannot become an evangelical minister because there is one doctrine held by the evangelical churches which I do not hold," he would have been honored for his fair dealing. Had he said to the orthodox church to which he belongs, "I do not believe that any human souls will be finally lost," his ingenuousness would have deserved and received a candid and Christian treatment by those directly concerned. But as the case now stands, he is not entitled to the credit that belongs to simplicity and godly sincerity. The latter fault is greater than the former. Perhaps he was not morally bound to assign the reason why he did not enter upon the preparation for the ministry. As he did not enter the ministry, he does not sail under false colors in this respect. But surely he is morally bound not to continue in his present church connections, while holding a tenet which the orthodox church regards as fatal error. At the very least, he is obligated to inform his fellow-members what his views are, and throw the responsibility of action upon them. As it now stands, he is assuming the responsibility himself, and is pretending to be what he is not.

This acknowledgment of a secret disbelief of one of the fundamental truths of Christianity while there is a public profession of belief in it, is very suggestive. It is valuable as a warning. The moral character of an individual rapidly deteriorates when he allows himself in any intellectual duplicity. If a man becomes a Universalist, and joins a Universalist society, though in the judgment of the orthodox he adopts a deadly error, he is yet an honest man. His sincerity is worthy of respect by the orthodox, and he can respect himself so far as this trait is concerned. But if a man becomes a Universalist and pretends still to be an evangelical believer, he must hold down his head in shame whenever he thinks of the part he is acting. Not only does he experience in his moral and religious character all the evil influence of the doctrinal error which he has adopted, but also all the demoralizing effects of insincerity and deception.

The writer of the article alluded to describes the mental perplexity and anguish which the doctrine of endless suffering has produced in his mind, and says that he " stays in the orthodox church because he is thoroughly orthodox in every other respect, and wishes to throw his influence on the side of the evangelical faith as a whole." Here we have an illustration of the confusion of mind that naturally accompanies the want of entire openness and sincerity. This writer thinks that he can be thoroughly orthodox in respect to the atonement of Christ, while asserting that the suffering from which it saves is only limited and transient; that he can have an evangelical hatred of sin while denying that it is eternally damnable; that he can receive all the teachings of Jesus Christ as infallible truth, and yet doubt the word of the Lord when he says, after a full and solemn delineation of the day of judgment and of his own office of judge, that those upon his left hand "shall go away into everlasting punishment." We have no time or space to present the Scripture proof for the doctrine of endless punishment. It is very probable that we could not by writing a volume convert the "Orthodox Disbeliever." But surely it cannot require much argument to prove that his present position is a false one. If his disbelief in endless punishment is right and proper, if the truth is really with him, he ought not to be where he is. He is in the wrong parish, and in the wrong pew. He ought to be opposing what he thinks to be error. He is now giving countenance to the doctrine of endless punishment. Belonging to an orthodox church and reciting an orthodox creed, all the weight of his influence goes to maintain a tenet which he says compelled Mrs. Marvyn, in the *Minister's Wooing*, to say : " There must be a mistake somewhere."

"ORTHODOX DISBELIEF" (AGAIN)

The writer of the article upon "Orthodox Disbelief," upon which we ventured a criticism, has sent us a private note which we can reply to only through the press. We assure our unknown correspondent that we have nothing but the best wishes for him, and that nothing moved us to discuss the subject which he first brought before the public, but a sincere desire to promote the cause of evangelical truth. We have no other motive in again calling attention to it, under the second stimulus of a letter from him.

Our correspondent in his private note explains his position more fully than he did in his published communication. From this latter we inferred that he held the doctrine of restoration, while professing to be an orthodox believer in the common doctrine of endless punishment. It appears now, that he believes in the annihilation of the wicked. We do not see that the question as to the uprightness of his position is essentially changed by this explanation. Orthodox churches find no more support in the Bible for the doctrine of annihilation than for that of restoration. One tenet is as thoroughly rejected by them as the other. A member of an orthodox church is understood to believe in the endless punishment of the impenitent. The orthodox interpretation of Scripture may be erroneous, as our correspondent asserts that it is, but this does not alter the fact that all orthodox churches stand before the world as committed to this interpretation, and all their members are committed with them. We submit, in all confidence, that our correspondent has not made his ecclesiastical position any less equivocal by this explanation.

Our correspondent says that years ago he spoke to his pastor of his " not *decided*, but preponderating faith in the eventual extinction of the impenitent, as being the teaching of the Bible;" that since that time he has " found many Christians in sympathy" with himself; and that "in necessary changes of abode, the need of expressing his doubts has not crossed his mind." We can understand how a wise and faithful pastor might think it best to allow a doubt respecting a cardinal truth, time to determine itself in one way or the other; especially in the instance of a church-member who had been religiously trained. But surely this ought not to have been seized upon as a sign that the pastor was himself inclined to the same doubt, and disposed to favor the error, or at least to wink at it. Is not our correspondent inferring too much from this pastor's forbearance and hopefulness? Neither ought he to make too much of the fact which he mentions, that "many Christians" sympathize with him. The term Christian, like the term Protestant, has come to be very wide and vague. Voltaire was a Protestant, and in the same sense all who are not Pagans and Mohammedans are Christians. The real question in this case is whether *orthodox* Christians sympathize with the doctrine of annihilation, and reject the doctrine of endless punishment.

The reason for not expressing his doubts respecting endless punishment which our correspondent finds in his changes of residence, strikes us as singular. We should have supposed that upon leaving one orthodox church and going to another, it would have been all the more natural and proper to inform the new parties with whom he proposed to unite in the profession of an orthodox creed, that there was one cardinal truth which he could not subscribe to. But if he felt no need of expressing his doubts privately, what was the need of publishing them in a newspaper, and giving them a circulation as wide as that of thistle-seeds in a high gale? When a person takes the responsibility of setting up his doubts in type, and giving them a currency among all classes of readers, he ought to be fully persuaded in his own mind, and not ashamed of his creed? Surely our correspondent is guilty of a grave inconsistency, to give it no harsher name, in combating anonymously in a public journal the doctrine of endless punishment as it is commonly received in orthodox churches, and then formally accepting the doctrine by remaining in the communion of an orthodox church. He does one thing under cover, and the contrary thing before the public.

The closing inquiry of our correspondent is this: "By what warrant is the doctrine of endless punishment made a test of church membership? Are orthodox believers prepared to reject all fellow-members who do not receive as undeniable revelation *their* interpretation of the Bible teaching on this question?" We answer that each church makes its own tests of membership, and from the nature of the case must do so. Who shall make the test for a church but the church itself? Would our correspondent have the Methodists draw up the creed of the Presbyterian Church, or vice versa? So long as there are various religious denominations there must be various creeds; and each creed must be the work of each denomination. And of all the articles which enter into the evangelical creeds, the doctrine of endless punishment is the one regarding which there is the least difference of opinion and statement. There are several views of the atonement, several views of original sin, and several views of election and predestination, but only one view of endless punishment. The Evangelical Alliance reduced the creed under which they would gather evangelical Protestantism, to as few articles as possible; but they retained the doctrine of endless punishment as indispensable to the integrity of an evangelical faith. And this answers the other inquiry of our correspondent. The evangelical churches of America and Europe and Asia, assembled in solemn and fraternal council, found the doctrine of endless punishment in the Word of God, as they understood and interpreted it. And they were " prepared to reject " communion with all who deny this doctrine. How could they do otherwise ? They do not force their interpretation of the Word of God upon any individual or any denomination. Neither do they affirm that their interpretation is infallible. But it is their solemn and religious conviction that their interpretation of the Bible on this point is correct. All who agree with them, they welcome. And all who disagree with them, they leave to their own freedom of will and of conscience. And now we ask, in closing, what would be thought of a body of men, or of a single man, who while privately rejecting the doctrine of endless punishment should publicly profess to believe it, and should join the Evangelical Alliance ?

ENDLESS PUNISHMENT AN ESSENTIAL DOCTRINE OF CHRISTIANITY

The assertion made recently in a religious journal, that "the fellowship of the churches may be safely extended to persons who do not believe in eternal punishment, provided they hold with cordial faith the essential truths of the evangelical system," proceeds upon the supposition that the doctrine of endless punishment is not an essential truth in the evangelical system. But the fact is, that there is no doctrine more necessary in order to the integrity of the evangelical system than that future punishment is eternal. Vicarious satisfaction for sin is the keystone of the arch of Christianity, and if endless retribution for sin be taken out, the whole scheme of redemption by the sufferings of Christ falls to the ground. Let us see if this is not so.

The Scriptures represent the sufferings and death of the Son of God as taking the place of the suffering and death due to the sinner for his sin, and in this way delivering him from his desert. But the sufferings of Christ, it is agreed by all

Trinitarians, from high Calvinists to low Arminians, are *infinite* in their dignity and value. They are the agony, not of a creature, but of incarnate God. All who are properly denominated "evangelical," though they may disagree upon many other points of doctrine, scout the notion that the sacrifice of Jesus Christ was merely finite, and that his blood possesses no higher expiating virtue than that of a creature. And in this they are supported by the Scriptures. But is it supposable that such an immense oblation as this would have been provided to redeem man from sin, if sin does not merit the immense penalty of eternal death, and is not to receive it? If sin is punishable and to be punished for only one thousand years, is it probable that one of the persons in the Trinity would submit to such an amazing humiliation as to become a worm of the dust, and undergo the awful passion of Calvary, in order to deliver his rebellious creature from a transient evil which is to be succeeded by billions of millenniums of happiness? A thousand years is indeed a long time, and a thousand years of suffering is indeed a great woe; but it shrinks to nothing in comparison with what is involved in the humiliation and agony of God incarnate. The profound Anselm puts this question to his pupil: "If the God-man were here present before you, and, you meanwhile having a full knowledge of his divine nature and character, it should be said, 'Unless you slay that Person, the whole world and the whole created universe will perish,' would you put him to death, in order to preserve the whole creation?" The pupil replies: "I would not, even if an infinite number of worlds were spread out before me." Anselm then puts this question to the pupil: "Suppose, again, that it were said to you: 'You must either slay this infinite Person, or the guilt and misery of all the sins of the world will come upon you?'" The pupil replies: "I would say, in answer, that I would sooner incur the aggravated guilt and misery of all the sins, past and future, of this world, and also of all the sin in addition that can possibly be conceived of, than incur the guilt of that one sin of slaying the Lord of glory." Now, if this is a correct reply in the case in which it is assumed that the punishment of sin is endless, much more would it be in case it is assumed that the punishment is only temporary. A suffering that in time would cease, surely would not justify such a strange and stupendous sacrifice as that of the only-begotten and well-beloved Son of God. We affirm therefore that the doctrine of Christ's atonement stands or falls with that of endless punishment. He who denies the latter must logically deny the former. He who subtracts anything from the demerit of man's sin, subtracts just so much from the merit of atoning blood. And what is true logically becomes true practically. Disbelievers in endless punishment are not believers in the atonement. Examine the mental history of one who lapses from an evangelical faith to infidelity, in any of its forms, and it will be found that the slide downward began first with doubts respecting man's responsibility for and the guilt of sin.

But a second and equally strong proof that the doctrine of endless punishment is necessary in order to the integrity of the evangelical system, is found in the fact that there can be no evangelical piety without it. Evangelical piety, all will concede, is characterized by penitence. This differentiates it from the piety of sentimentalism, of rationalism, and of pantheism, for all these have their varieties of piety. He who is destitute of the publican's feeling when he cried, "God, be merciful to me a sinner," does not possess the piety of the gospel. He is impenitent. Now, we affirm that he who in his heart denies and rejects the doctrine of endless punishment, does not and cannot truly repent of sin. We know that there are some theologians like Müller and Dorner whose general evangelical character will not be denied, who hold the error of restoration, namely, that a part of mankind are saved in the middle state, and these are cited in proof of the position that a belief in endless punishment is not essential to belief in Christ. But this class of theologians do not assert that sin does not *merit* eternal suffering. On the contrary, they affirm that it does in its own nature, and that irrespective of the death of Christ it will certainly meet an endless penalty. But they think that in the future world the atonement of Christ will be applied to many of the human family, and that a second probation will save men upon the same principles, and by the same method, as the first. This heresy stands upon its own bottom, and need not be refuted here. But it is plain that such theologians as these cannot be cited in support of the tenet that sin does not *deserve* endless punishment, and therefore will not receive it.

Every man who has truly repented, has confessed in his heart to God that he is hell-deserving. Every one who really puts his trust for acquittal at the bar of God in the atonement of Jesus Christ, implicitly and virtually acknowledges that his sin merits the worm that dieth not, and the fire that is not quenched. The depth and strength of the believer's conviction upon this point vary. Some are more poignantly convinced of the turpitude of sin than others; but no true believer in Christ ever positively denies that he might justly be punished for ever and ever. To perceive the truth of this assertion, let us suppose the contrary. Suppose that a person under religious concern should say to his pastor: " I know that I am a sinner; I confess that I have often done wrong; but I do not believe that I deserve, for the sins of this short life, to be punished everlastingly." Would that pastor dare to tell him that his experience of sin was "evangelical?" On the contrary, would he not bid him, most earnestly and solemnly, search his heart yet more thoroughly, under the light of God's Spirit and truth, until he should melt down in a really contrite manner, and say, what every true penitent says:

> " My lips with shame my sins confess,
> Against Thy law, against Thy grace;

Lord, should Thy judgment grow severe,
I am condemned, but Thou art clear.

" Should sudden vengeance seize my breath,
I must pronounce Thee just in death ;
And if my soul were sent to hell,
Thy righteous law approves it well.

" Yet save a trembling sinner, Lord,
Whose hope, still hovering round Thy word,
Would light on some sweet promise there,
Some sure support against despair."

This is evangelical penitence, and nothing that comes short of it is worthy of the name, or will prove to be the thing, when all sinners shall stand at the bar of God, and know even as they are known.

HELLPHOBIA

In a book entitled "Notes on Paris," written by Taine to describe the spirit and manners of modern Babylon, there is an allusion to some of the religious phenomena of American life. The author says that at a Methodist camp-meeting "a platform is raised, and a half dozen preachers take turns in preaching upon predestination and damnation and other equally agreeable topics. They relieve each other in describing the agony of the sinner, his death, the progress of corruption, the fires of hell, and all the details of the broiling." That predestination is one of the topics of Methodist preaching will be news upon this side of the Atlantic, but accuracy is hardly to be expected from a source which "like the French all clinquant" (Henry VIII., i., 1) must be brilliant or it is nothing.

We have quoted this scurrilous passage as a specimen of what may be denominated "hellphobia," in order to analyze a kind of fear which shows itself in a certain species of literature, and in a certain class of persons.

A worldly and wicked man is afraid of the future life and of the future retribution, with that kind of perturbation which is of the nature of fright. The thought of sudden death produces consternation in his mind. The apprehension that after all there may be in reserve for him a searching examination into the deeds which he has done in the body, affects him very much as the cry of fire at midnight does. He is put into a panic. This accounts for the *irritability* with which the doctrine of hell is met by literary men of the calibre and character of Taine. If there were an absolute disbelief, and an utter absence of all anxiety about what happens to man at death, this tenet of Christianity would be dismissed with a serene indifference. A Protestant is never irritated by the doctrine of the immaculate conception of the Virgin, or of the Pope's infallibility. He has no kind of belief in them, and the statement and defence of them awakens no excited feeling of any sort. He cannot be made angry at them. And the case would be the same with the infidel and the doctrine of endless punishment, if there were the same utter unbelief. But the case is different. The "looking-for of judgment and fiery indignation" is native to man. The sceptic, notwithstanding his denial of immortality, sometimes fears that he may be an immortal being, and that there may be future punishment of sin. This fear worries him, and he takes every opportunity to ridicule and combat what he fears. He whistles to keep his courage up. He has hellphobia, and it shows itself in an irascible temper and an exasperated phraseology, whenever the frightful subject is brought to his mind.

This same spurious and servile fear of hell is seen in some preachers. They take pains to sneer at the orthodox view of future punishment, to ridicule that religious experience which has solemnity in it, and to recommend a mirthful piety. From their manner of treating the subject, it is plain that they fear hell more than they fear sin. Hell, for them, is the most dreadful theme that can be brought before the human mind, and they too, like Taine, are made irritable by it. They, too, have hellphobia.

A Christian believer is not so. A thorough-going orthodox man is not afraid of hell in this panic style. His dread of everlasting banishment from God, and from all that is pure and good, is too well considered and too profound to throw him into a mere fright. He is calm and thoughtful in the matter. He obeys the command to "fear him who when he hath killed hath power to cast into hell," in a rational and intelligent way. And because he fears hell in this true and solemn manner, he has made preparation to escape it, in the way arranged and pointed out by Almighty God himself.

The amiable Channing objects to the orthodox view of hell, that if one really believed the doctrine he could not have a moment of mental serenity. He would run from house to house and from man to man, entreating them to flee from the wrath to come. He would not be able either to eat, drink, or sleep. In short, life for a believer, upon the orthodox theory, would be a paroxysm.

That the Church is not sufficiently in earnest in warning sinners, and endeavoring to save them, will be granted by the Church itself in sorrow and penitence. But it does not follow that a deep and solemn dread of hell, such as the Bible enjoins, is incompatible with mental serenity or mental happiness. Christ came to save from hell, and he who is in Christ believes as religiously as ever that there is a hell, but rejoices that a ransom has been found that "saves from going down into the pit." The believer, consequently, can both fear and rejoice together. He can rejoice with fear and trembling, as he is commanded to do. He can fear and rejoice with reference to his own welfare, and he can do the same with reference to the welfare of his fellow-men towards whom he has been faithful.

We remark, in conclusion, that the sceptic's hellphobia is far more to be dreaded than the Christian's fear of hell. Fright is the worst form of apprehension. It is useless, besides being tormenting. It does not deliver from peril, or in any way help to do so. A frightened child or man is almost certain to be lost. He is too much excited to use his limbs, and sinks under the waves as helpless as a paralytic. In like manner, that man who is in a constant panic about hell, and is irritated by the mention or preaching of it, will make no efforts to be saved from it. He will experience all that is wearing and depressing in the doctrine, and will feel none of those salutary influences that may be made to issue from it. He will die of hellphobia, as one is sure to die of hydrophobia.

THE SINNER AT REST

A DAILY journal, in an obituary sketch, describes the subject of it in these terms: "His nature was diseased with arrogance, passion, and cruelty. In youth and early manhood, he was boisterous, sensual, revengeful, and profligate. In age, he was misanthropical. Of self-poise, conscious rectitude, patience, and meek submission, he did not possess a particle." After this delineation, the writer proceeds in these words: "He has long been a wreck. There was nothing before him here but an arid waste of suffering, and since we understand him thus, we cannot but think, with a tender gratitude, that at last he is beyond the reach of all trouble, and where neither care, sorrow, self-rebuke, unreasoning passion, resentment against the world, nor physical pain can any more torment him."

We do not know whether this description of character is correct. We neither affirm nor deny its accuracy, because we are in total ignorance. But upon the supposition that the journalist has rightly described his subject, we affirm that his judgment respecting the final issue and result of such a life is a very high-handed and bold procedure. For if the New Testament is true, and the words of Jesus Christ respecting the last judgment are authoritative, sin and sensuality have a totally different end from this. According to the Scriptures, the passions and lusts of man do not, like the winds and hurricanes of the tropics, rage themselves into rest. If he who claims to be the Redeemer of man knew whereof he affirmed, the working of evil desire, occurring as it does in the immortal nature of a responsible creature, goes on for evermore. By what right and authority, then, does a mortal man, whose breath is in his nostrils, and who never was in the other world, and knows nothing from personal observation of what goes on there—by what right does he reverse the statements of the Founder of the Christian religion and assert that there is peace for the wicked? We know that the estimate which the secular press puts upon its own judgments and knowledge is extravagant, but we can hardly believe that, in the calmness of reflection, any journalist would seriously claim a knowledge of the life beyond this, and of the condition of departed spirits, that is superior to that of Jesus of Nazareth. And yet such a judgment as the above quoted implies such a claim. We submit that this is a very bold and high-handed procedure.

But it is more than this. It is an immoral and vicious procedure. It is adjusting a creed to the passions of men. It is constructing a theory of the future life in accordance not with what is lovely and of good report, but with what is vile and degrading. To tell a man that drunkenness and debauchery, like the violent physical exertion of a storm-tossed sailor, will end in a deep and restful sleep, is to promise happiness to sin. It is to tell the transgressor that the wages of sin is life. Such teaching contradicts all ethics that are respectable, either pagan or Christian. And its influence upon the individual and society is utterly demoralizing. No social virtue can live if such a theory shall prevail. In some aspects, he who broaches such a theory is more immoral than the drunkard or the debauchee. His vice is mental. The drunkard, though enslaved by his own action to his own voluntary indulgence, may not, nevertheless, have changed his creed or vitiated his ethics. In the moments of reflection, after his debauch is over, he may still see and believe with trembling, that no drunkard shall inherit the kingdom of God. The head is still right, though the heart is wrong. But here is a fellow-man, whose cooler blood or lymphatic temperament has, perchance, kept him from vice, who stands beside the wretched slave of appetite and tells him that his sin shall wear itself out, and that all shall be peaceful with him at last.

The journal from which we have made the quotation which has led to these remarks complains of the fearful depravity of this city, so prolific in violence and crime, and also of the still more startling proof of this depravity in that this violence and crime goes unpunished. We tell this journalist that he will be held responsible for this crime and this inefficiency in the execution of law, just so far as his theory that God will not punish sin in hell prevails. The secular newspaper, to a great extent, forms public sentiment in the lower and middle classes of society. The educated and cultivated class derive their opinions from books and literature proper. But this class is a minority, and in a country governed by universal suffrage must always possess but little actual power in the election of judges, and the making and executing of laws. Hence the secular press, if it disseminates a false theory of crime, or a false view of sin and punishment, becomes a potent instrument of evil. Its opinions, like water through a swamp, percolate through the whole substratum of community, and make it rotten and sour.

The existing demoralization in society and politics, in this city, is due, mainly, to a disbelief of the doctrine of endless punishment. Men cease to fear future misery, and then they fear nothing else. Reputation, health, and even the happiness of friends and family are not sufficient to prevent the embezzlement of trust-funds, or the indulgence of sensual appetites. Nothing but the apprehension of endless pain after death can put a restraint upon human passion, and even this is not a certain preventive. It is, however, the strongest of motives except those of grace and love, and whenever its pressure is taken off, all other merely prudential motives prove to be bands of tow before the flame. If, therefore, this journalist does, in very truth, mourn over the existing dissoluteness of morals, and insecurity of life and property, and would do something towards its removal, let him not say to that numerous and unreflecting class for whom he writes that sin is at rest when the mortal coil is shuffled off. On the contrary, let him stand in good company, and with Plato and Plutarch, of the Pagans, and with Shakespeare and Bacon, of the Christians, tell the dissolute and the vicious of that "fearful something after death."

ALL RELIGIONS NOT EQUALLY VALUABLE

MAX MÜLLER delivered an instructive and interesting course of lectures before the Royal Institution upon the Science of Religion. The fourth and concluding one draws two conclusions, prepared for by the preceding lectures: 1. That "there is no religion which does not contain some grains of truth;" and, 2. That "in one sense every religion was a true religion; being the only religion which was possible at the time; which was compatible with the language, the thoughts, and the sentiments of each generation; which was appropriate to the age of the world." The first of these propositions no one would dispute. It is a remark of St. Augustine himself, which Müller quotes. But the second is not true, except in the sense not intended by the author, that every one of the pantheistic or polytheistic religions was the only one "possible at the time" *because of the sinfulness of its adherents*, and the only one "compatible" *with their evil thoughts and sentiments*. In all that this learned and serious writer says respecting the amount of true morality that is taught in the systems of Confucius, Zoroaster, Buddha, and the writings of Plato, Aristotle, and Cicero, he will carry the judgment even of the believer in the pre-eminence of Christianity over all other religions. There has probably been a tendency among some Christian writers to under-estimate and misstate natural religion, for the purpose of exalting revealed. This volume of Müller will do good service in correcting this error, and in thereby indirectly supporting the position of St. Paul, that the heathen are without excuse, because they know enough of the true God and human duty to make them guilty for not worshipping the true God, and not doing their duty.

It is just here that the work of Müller is defective, and teaches serious error. Because a man knows his duty, it does not follow that he *performs* it. A heathen, like a nominal Christian, may have a very good theory, and be guilty of very bad practice. "I see the good," said a pagan, "and follow the bad." The generations of men, under the lead of their sages and philosophers, had many lessons of wisdom and virtue taught them, but this does not prove that they practised them. Did the Athenian people obey the teachings of Socrates? Do the millions of China practise the excellent precept of Confucius, quoted by Müller, and quoted over and over again by very different men from him, for the purpose of detracting from the originality of Christ's golden rule: "What you do not like when done to yourself, do not do that to others"? Turn to the dialogues of Plato, and read those serious and earnest statements of the dying Socrates respecting the vanity of time and sense, the dignity and importance of truth and virtue, and ask Müller, or any other theorist, whether these teachings exerted the least influence upon the sensual and pleasure-loving populace of Athens. All who heard them, or heard of them, could not but assent to their truthfulness, but none gave heed to them.

Hence Müller is guilty of a fallacy, when, from the correct premise, that all the religions of the globe contain some elements of moral truth, he draws the conclusion that those who lived under these religions *obeyed* this truth. "I suppose," he says, "that most of us, sooner or later in life, have felt how the whole world—this wicked world, as we call it—is changed by magic, if once we can make up our mind to give men credit for good motives, never to be suspicious, never to think evil, never to think ourselves better than our neighbors. Trust a man to be true and good, and even if he is not, your trust will tend to make him true and good. It is the same with the religions of the world. Let us but make up our mind to look in them for what is true and good, and we shall hardly know our old religion again. If they are the work of the devil, as many of us have been brought up to believe, then never was there a kingdom so divided against itself from the very beginning. There is no religion —or, if there is, I do not know it—which does not say : ' Do good, avoid evil.' There is none which does not contain what Rabbi Hillel called the quintessence of all religions, the simple warning,

'Be good, my boy.'" Now, we put our finger upon this tenet of the Rabbi, and upon the other contained, says our author in all religions, and ask him, Are they *obeyed?* And if not, what then is the position before God and justice of every heathen man? It is one thing to look into the pagan religions and find some things true and good in *them*, and quite another thing to look into the pagan *heart* and find it full of "fornication, uncleanness, lasciviousness, idolatry, witchcraft, hatred, variance, emulations, wrath, strife, seditions, envyings, murders, drunkenness, revellings, and such like." Gal. 5 : 20, 21. Instead of inferring, as Müller does, that because the generations of men had these religions which contain so much sound ethics, saying to men, "Obey the voice of conscience; fear God and love your neighbor," therefore they did obey and all is well with them, and the doctrine of their eternal perdition is an excrescence upon Christianity as the worship of Moloch was an excrescence upon the ancient religion (we quote his own statement)—instead of this inference, we put it to our readers whether the exact contrary does not follow? If the heathen world has had such an amount of truth in the Vedas and Zend-Avesta, and other systems, and has *disobeyed* it, then they stand upon the same footing with every inhabitant of Christendom who has known his duty by the light of a clearer revelation, and has not lived in accordance with it. If, therefore, there be condemnation in the day of judgment and a punishment in eternity for the latter, is there not also, in less degree it is true, but with as much certainty, for the former?

The good maxims of Confucius and the Vedas, and the yet higher ethics and truer philosophy of Plato and Aristotle, do not prove that the millions of China, India, Greece, and Rome were prepared for a pure and holy heaven, any more than the existence of the decalogue in Christendom proves that all the millions who have composed Christendom in the past are now safe and blessed in eternity. "Not the mere *hearers* of the law shall be pronounced righteous, but the *doers* of the law." Müller, and others like him, are, in fact, terrible preachers of damnation, when their doctrine is run out for them to its logical results. For if the heathen possesses this great amount of religious truth and knowledge, it must be that holy justice will punish him in case he has not conformed his character and conduct to it. And how many heathen have done this?

The endeavor of the natural religionist to find salvation for the heathen in the ethics of their religions, is the old and standing attempt of human nature *to find salvation by the works of the law* instead of by faith in the Divine mercy revealed in Christ. Theorists of this class, of whom there are many among the present writers on Comparative Religions, blink the fact that all the natural religions of the globe are *law*, not *gospel*. They teach morality, but make no provision for the pardon and extirpation of immorality. They say to man, "Be good," but do not make him so. They waken remorse of conscience, but do nothing to pacify it. They announce a law native to the human constitution that condemns the transgressor, but leave him to its condemnation. To find mental peace and eternal life for sinful men in such a merely legal and non-pardoning religion as this, is to find acquittal for a criminal in the law that sentences him, and inward tranquillity in the sense of duty which he has violated. This contradiction is tacitly acknowledged in the general denial by this class of writers of the fact of *sin*, and the assertion of the substantial goodness of human nature. If, as Müller says, "we can make up our minds to give men credit for good motives," and can "trust [believe] a man to be true and good even if he is not," it will then be possible to believe that "the works of the law," as St. Paul calls them, or natural goodness, as the moralist denominates them, are a sufficient preparation for eternal existence beyond the grave. But if the Biblical account of the condition of man be adopted, and he is held to be in a state of depravity and condemnation because of his violation of the law of *his own conscience*, then the expiation of sin by the vicarious sacrifice of the Son of God, and its eradication by regeneration by the Holy Spirit, afford the only ground of hope. Such is St. Paul's account of the Greek and Roman ethical systems, which were purer than those of Egypt, India, and China. He declares that the holiness and justice of God are plainly taught in them, but denies that his saving mercy is. "The wrath of God," he says, "is revealed from heaven against all ungodliness," in the human constitution and thereby in all the pagan religions; but the revelation of the compassion of God towards sinners he confines to Christianity.[1]

If it be objected that St. Paul declares that "God hath made of one blood all nations of men, for to dwell on all the face of the earth, that they should seek the Lord if haply they might feel after him and find him," and that missionary records mention instances in which an unevangelized pagan was found with a humble sense of sin, and a longing after Him who is "the Desire of all nations," the reply is, that this phenomenon is not the effect of ethnic religion but of Divine grace overflowing into paganism. It results from the inward operation of that Holy Spirit "who worketh when, and where, and how he pleaseth." Honor to whom honor is due. The transforming power by which a heathen obtains the contrite spirit of the prodigal son, cannot be ascribed to the moral precepts of Socrates, Confucius, and Sakyamuni. The Holy Ghost may and does employ "the law written on the heart," and rewritten by the heathen sage in his moral system, as a means of conviction of sin, and may follow this with the regeneration of the soul, but this regeneration is due to revealed religion which is gospel,

[1] Not long ago a young Brahmin of India came to the house of a missionary seeking an interview. In the course of conversation he said: "Many things which Christianity contains I find in Hindooism; but there is one thing which Christianity has and Hindooism has not." "What is that?" the missionary asked. His reply was striking: "A Saviour."

not to natural religion which is only law. The salvation of man depends upon the new-birth. "Except a man be born again, he cannot see the kingdom of God." It also depends upon the actual existence of a pure heart. "Without holiness no man shall see the Lord." Neither the new heart nor the pure heart can be originated by the ethical method of mere command. *Life* and not law is needed for this. There is nothing of a *redemptive* nature in the teachings of the Hindoo and Grecian sages. The renovation of an unevangelized man can no more be ascribed to the good ethics of an ethnic religion, than that of an evangelized man can be to the still better ethics of the decalogue. In this respect the ten commandments are as helpless as the ethnic religions. They cannot extirpate sin, any more than can the purest maxims of Plato, Aristotle, and Gautama. It is not the law, written or unwritten, that forgives sin and changes the character. "By the law is the knowledge of sin," not its pardon. "The law is the strength of sin" for a sinner, not its destruction. "When the commandment came, sin revived and I died." "If there had been a law given which could have given life, verily righteousness should have been by the law." "The law made nothing perfect, but the bringing in of a *better hope* did." These Scripture declarations concerning the utter impotence of mere law and ethics when confronted with the guilt and resistance of human nature, are verified by the actual facts. No guilt is pardoned, and no moral corruption is eradicated, by the legal method. The populations of India and China, like those of Greece and Rome, have been unmoved from generation to generation by the wisdom of their sages. This ethics has not been put in practice, and has brought no peace with God. Will any one contend that that moral philosophy which Bacon calls "the heathen divinity" has been the actuating and transforming principle for heathendom, as the gospel of Christ has been for Christendom? On the contrary, has not the moral truth inlaid in the human conscience, and enunciated in the systems of the heathen sages, been "held down in unrighteousness," as St. Paul affirms; and have not the character and conduct of the vast masses of heathenism, from time immemorial, been as contrary to the doctrines of natural morality as of revealed religion? The moral law detects and condemns sin, the world over, but this is all it can do. Like lunar caustic, it bites into the mortified flesh and shows the nature of the disease, but there is no healing virtue in it. "It is," says Owen ("Saint's Perseverance," Ch. x.), "the Spirit of Christ alone that hath sovereign power in our souls, of killing and making alive. As no man quickeneth his own soul, so no man by the power of any threatenings of the law can kill his own sin. There was never a single sin truly mortified by the law. All that the law can do of itself, is but to entangle sin, and thereby irritate and provoke it, like a bull in a net, or a beast dragged to the slaughter."

CHRISTIANITY ALONE IS ABLE TO INCLINE A MAN

When Henry Martyn was carrying the Gospel into Mohammedan countries, he was frequently told by the Moollahs that his religion was no better than theirs, because the Koran commands the practice of the cardinal virtues as do the Christian Scriptures. The Brahmin makes the same objection to the missionary of the present day, when he asserts that the Vedas enjoin upon their readers the worship of one supreme God. The New England Brahmin, Emerson, also, in a recent lecture, sets the Christian religion upon the same level with that of Confucius, because the Chinese sage taught the "golden rule." Martyn replied to the Mohammedan unbeliever, by saying that "Jesus Christ came not so much to teach, as to *die*." His chief office was not so much that of a sage as that of a priest. Men needed not so much a teacher who should instruct them in their duty, as a sacrifice that should atone for their failure to do their duty. This reply of Martyn would have little force for one who denies that sin needs atonement, and we will not, therefore, press it in reference to this class of persons. But there is another aspect of Christ and his gospel, which even the unbeliever in the doctrine of atonement must feel the force of.

Suppose it to be true (which, however, we deny) that Confucius did teach the "golden rule" as clearly and fully as Christ taught it in the Sermon on the Mount, would this make Confucius equal to Jesus Christ? It would so far as this particular rule is concerned, provided that Christ did no more than merely *teach* the rule. But he did and still does a great deal more than this. *He imparts a disposition to obey the rule.* This Confucius never did while on earth, and has never done since he left it. It is easy enough to point to the north star; any child can do this. But to carry a human being to the north star, is beyond the power of man. When Christ said to a paralytic, "Arise, take up thy bed and walk," he empowered him to the act. He imparted a vital force which enabled the patient to do what he was commanded to do, and without which he could not have done it. But when natural religion says to the moral paralytic, "Do right," "Be perfect," it bestows no spiritual power along with the command, and hence it accomplishes nothing.

It is surprising to see how this great difference between Christianity and all the natural religions of the globe is overlooked, in the contest which is now going on. The "liberal" treatises on Comparative Religion invariably ignore it. The utmost that Confucius and Socrates can do, is to give good advice. They cannot *incline* and *enable* men to obey it. Socrates confesses this with sadness. It is the burden of his soul that men will not hear, and that he has no power to move their hearts. But Christ possesses this marvellous power. He can not only say to men, "Whatsoever ye would that men should do to you, do ye even so to them," but he can actually induce them to do it. Men for centuries, of all grades of civilization and culture, have come under the power of the gospel, and have found in themselves a new heart. This is not theory, but fact. That Christianity possesses this wonderful power of spiritual transformation is as certain as that magnetism affects iron. It is demonstrable by actual experience and observation.

St. Paul, speaking of the superiority of the gospel above the moral law, remarks that "if there had been a law given which could have given life, verily righteousness should have been by the law." Now, this *imparting of moral life* is precisely what no religion but that of Christ is competent to. If the human heart could have been inclined and persuaded to practise the "golden rule" by the religion of Confucius, then verily there would have been some color of reason for the assertion that Confucius and Christ are equals. But the human heart in China remains the same selfish and self-seeking thing, and is filled with the same ill-will from generation to generation, until the missionary preaches the religion of that redeeming God who says, "A new heart will I give you, and a new spirit will I put within you; and I will take away the stony heart out of your flesh, and I will give you an heart of flesh." There is not a religion upon the globe, excepting the religion of the Old and New Testaments, that has ever made a saint out of a sinner. There are many religions that have advised and commanded men to be better and to do better, but they have never gone beyond advice and command.

The same reasoning applies to that other great truth which is taught by some of the natural religions, namely, the unity of God. No religion but the Christian inclines and enables man to love and serve this one God. It is not enough merely to know and believe that there is one only supreme God. The devils, says St. James, believe this. If the Vedas should teach monotheism as distinctly as does the Old Testament, this would not be sufficient for man's needs. To supply all his wants, it would be necessary that they should so transform him in the spirit of his mind, that God should be the object of his affection and worship. But they have not done this for a single Hindoo, and they never will. Yet thousands of Hindoos by the gospel have been made new creatures. The test, therefore, to be applied to any religion is, not what it tells man to do, but what it tells and *inclines* him to do. There is but one religion in which God says to the lost world of mankind, "This is the covenant that I will make with the house of Israel; I will put my laws into their mind, and write them in their hearts; for I will be merciful to their unrighteousness, and their sins and their iniquities will I remember no more." Heb. 8: 10, 12.

THE REASON WHY SIN SHOULD BE FORGIVEN

The patriarch Job, in the depth of his distress, cries out, "O that I knew where I might find God! that I might come even to his seat! I would order my cause before him, and fill my mouth with arguments." An argument is some good and sufficient reason why something should be granted or done. Whoever has one, may expect to obtain what he asks for. He who can assign a reason why his request should be allowed hopes to succeed, but he who can specify no ground for his request has small expectation of receiving anything.

This general principle holds good in all provinces in which man acts. In case he would get anything from his fellow-man, he must have good and sufficient reasons. Whoever makes a request of his neighbor, or even of his friend, will hear the inquiry, Why should I do it? What reason can you give me for doing it? But still more is this the case in the higher province of religion. God is eminently a Being of reason, and he never acts without grounds and motives of action. Whenever, therefore, a man would obtain anything from his Maker, he must fill his mouth with arguments. He must be able to assign a valid reason why God should do the thing he asks for.

But what arguments has man, and what reasons can he give, when he comes before his Maker for blessings? Are there any that spring out of himself? Has he done anything for God which he can mention as a sufficient reason why God should now do something for him? Take the daily bread, for example, for which he prays. What man upon the planet has so worked for God, and done him a service, that the daily bread would be a fair and just equivalent? Take the man's life itself, his very existence. What has he accomplished in the way of honor, benefit, or service, of any kind toward God, which constitutes a sufficient reason why God should continue his existence for even an hour? The fact is that if a man looks into himself, into his own doings and deservings, he cannot find a scintilla of a reason why God should give him either his daily subsistence or his daily existence. Everything that he has, even life, breath, and all things pertaining to life, come to him from his Maker. The wealth which he may have accumulated is the gift of God; for no man ever became rich in spite of Divine providence. In looking around, therefore, for arguments wherewith to appear before God, and upon the strength of which to ask a blessing from him, man must go out of and beyond himself.

But all this is still more true of man as a *sinner*. If he cannot find any sufficient reason in his own doings and deservings why God should give him his daily bread, still less can he find in them the reason why God should bestow upon him the forgiveness of sins. Man can no more merit spiritual blessings than he can merit temporal good. He is, if possible, even more dependent upon the Divine mercy, than he is upon the Divine omnipotence.

When, therefore, a guilty creature, like man, seeks a reason why he should be forgiven he must look away, entirely, from himself. And the argument with which he must appear before God, is the *atonement* of the Son of God. This is a valid and sufficient reason why his sin should be blotted out. On a dark and gloomy Sunday, we went into St. Margaret's church, hard by Westminster Abbey, and heard a sermon by a young minister of the Church of England. It was a plain and powerful discourse upon the atonement addressed to some twenty or thirty hearers, mostly old women of the godly sort. Among other striking and truthful utterances, this was one: "Jesus Christ is the *hold* which the sinner has upon God." This sentence is the gospel in a nutshell. By pleading the merits of Christ's oblation, the sinful creature, utterly powerless in himself, becomes almighty with God. For in so doing he brings an argument to bear upon the infinite justice and the infinite mercy that is omnipotent. Whoever lifts up the prayer, "Blot out my transgressions because Christ has died for them on the cross," assigns a reason why that prayer should be granted, and a reason which God himself knows to be valid and good, because He himself has provided it.

It is here that the fatal error of Socinianism is apparent. Socinus, like all who reject the doctrine of vicarious atonement, asks for the remission of sins without assigning a reason for the procedure. He brings no argument when he appears before God. He simply says, "Forgive me." The evangelical forgiveness is forgiveness with a reason; it is a rational compassion. The Socinian forgiveness is forgiveness without a reason, and is consequently an irrational mercy. No man can be certain that his prayer for the remission of sins will be granted, if he approaches God in this manner. Guilt is always doubtful, and needs something to assure it when it appears before the tribunal of justice, which is also the seat of mercy. This great assurance is furnished to guilty man in the satisfaction of the Son of God. If he makes mention of this, he finds that he can stand, guilty as he is, before the Holy One. But if he ignores this, if he is silent upon this point, and especially if he positively denies and rejects this divine provision, he comes before God without any argument at all, and assigns no good reason why his prayer should be heard. Suppose that after he has uttered the supplication, "Forgive me my sins," a voice from heaven should answer, "Why should they be forgiven?" He must be speechless. No answer can be made to that inquiry but the answer, "Because the Son of God has died on the cross, the just for the unjust." And he whose heart does not prompt him to return this answer to this question of questions, and especially he whose heart is hostile to this answer, and would assign some other reason—perhaps his good works, perhaps his sufferings and penances—will find himself to be like the guest in our Lord's parable, who went to the marriage without a wedding garment. "When the king came in to see the guests, he saw there a man which had not on the wedding garment: and he saith unto him, Friend, how camest thou hither not having a wedding garment? And he was speechless."

ADVICE TO THE INQUIRING SINNER

It is not right or safe to depart from the method prescribed in the Scriptures for an anxious soul to take in order to salvation. Even a slight deviation, however well intended, works mischief. We have heard during seasons of religious awakening, the inquirer exhorted to "give his heart to God," to "submit to God," to "resolve to serve Christ." This is not the direction which Paul gave to the anxious jailer, and neither does it agree with the declarations of our Lord respecting the particular kind of act which man must perform in order to salvation. The Jews once came to the Redeemer asking what they must do to work the works of God, and his reply was, "This is the work of God, that ye *believe* on him whom he hath sent." The first act for the soul in order to salvation is the act of faith. "Believe on the Lord Jesus Christ," is the first and only direction, therefore, which should be given to an inquiring sinner. When this has been done, other things will follow naturally, and be done in their order and place; but until it has been done, not a step toward heaven can be taken.

There are objections to the other direction to which we have alluded, which we will specify.

In the first place, when an inquiring person is bidden to give his heart to God, he is commanded to *present* something to God, instead of being invited to receive something from him. The gospel method is thus wholly reversed. The Scripture representation of the way of salvation indisputably makes it, from first to last, a blessing which comes down from God to man. It does not go up from man to God. "Ask and ye shall receive." Christ is appointed "to give both faith and repentance," as well as the remission of sins. Even the very first exercises of sorrow for sin, and the very first and faintest exercise of faith, are wrought by God. When, therefore, a sinful man is bidden, as the first act upon his part, to give his heart to God, he is converted from a recipient of salvation to an agent and author of it. He is urged to do a "work" as the very first thing in the process. And it is a work which is the most difficult of performance, for a helpless and guilt-smitten sinner, that can be conceived of. In reality, the whole immense burden is thrown upon the poor despairing soul, in the very outset. He is told that if he will give his heart to God, if he will submit his will to Christ, his salvation is assured. But this is to put in the fore-front of the religious experience something which does not belong there. No man can surrender and sweetly submit his heart to God, unless he believes that the blood of Jesus Christ cleanses from all sin.

We are not speaking, of course, of the succession in time. The two things may not be distinguishable in time measured by the clock, but in the order of nature the soul must first accept and receive Christ as its atonement before God, before it can become subject and submissive to his will. And, therefore, this act of faith must be urged upon the inquirer first of any, and before any other act is spoken of or enjoined.

In the second place, this direction *conceals* Christ and his sacrificial work from the guilt-smitten soul. While it is engaged in the attempt to overcome the love of self, and to give itself wholly to God, it cannot see the cross, because, if for no other reason, it is too much absorbed. It is looking within, instead of looking out and away to the Lamb of God. It is summoning its energies to overcome its own self-love, and subdue its obstinate aversion to holiness, instead of sending up an imploring and believing glance to the merciful Redeemer who "of God is made unto it wisdom, and righteousness, and sanctification." The true answer to the sinner's inquiry, "What shall I do?" is, to say to him, "Do nothing; only believe." But if the answer that is given be the one which we are criticising; if he be told to give his heart to God; he is bidden to "do," and this will prevent his "believing." No one can do two things at once; and if the anxious inquirer be straining every muscle to its utmost tension in order to subdue his native depravity, how can he relax every muscle and in helpless impotence cast himself upon Christ? We cannot open and shut the hand in one and the same instant, and by one and the same volition. Our Lord affirms that his yoke is easy. It is so, because the act of faith is not a strenuous and vehement act, but a trusting and recipient one. It does not try to originate holiness by its own volition, but it longs to receive the holiness which is freely given it of God. The eye and not the hand is the member of the body which the Holy Spirit has chosen, by which to explain the act by which salvation is secured. *Look* unto me, and be ye saved. *Behold* the Lamb of God. We are not to raise the hand and lift at a burden; we are not to raise the foot and run a long and severe race; but we are simply to open the eye and gaze steadily upon the atoning Christ, dying a sacrifice for our guilt. It is indeed true that after faith has come, after the soul has beheld the cross, after the eye has performed its function, the hand and the foot and all the members of the body come into requisition. Having accepted and received Christ by faith, and having thereby been delivered from condemnation, the soul is then to run a race, and fight a fight, and carry a burden. But the previous faith makes all this activity easy and successful. When the eye has seen the Lord, it is easy then to lift the hand for him. Faith works by love, and the love of Christ constraineth us.

In giving advice, therefore, to inquiring souls, we should not direct their attention, first of all, to the *results* of faith in Christ, but to faith itself.

The surrender of the heart to God, entire submission to his will, a steady and strong determination to obey the commandments of Christ, renunciation of the world as the chief good—these fruits of belief on the Lord Jesus Christ ought to be kept in the background while the soul is urged, first of all, and as the one thing needful, to cast itself humbly and penitently upon the atoning work of the Son of God. There is no danger of undervaluing the consequences of faith, by thus laying stress upon faith in the outset; for only from faith as the root can all these consequences spring. He who has believed on the Lord Jesus Christ finds that in so doing he has given his heart to God as the natural result. But he who attempts to give his heart to God, before he has believed on the Son of God, is attempting an impossibility, and that too by a dead lift.

There are two invitations given by the Lord Jesus Christ, which cover the whole subject of a sinner's salvation. One is an invitation to come *to* him, and the other an invitation to come *after* him. Examples of the first are: "Come unto me all ye that are weary and heavy laden, and I will give you rest." Matt. 11:28. "All that the Father giveth me shall come to me; and him that cometh to me I will in no wise cast out." John 6:37. Examples of the second are: "Take my yoke upon you, and learn of me, for I am meek and lowly in heart." Matt. 11:29. "If any man will come after me, let him deny himself, and take up his cross, and follow me." Matt. 16:24.

The first of these is an invitation to come *to* the Saviour, by trusting penitently in his atoning blood in order to pardon and reconciliation with God's holiness. The second is an invitation to come *after* the Saviour, by imitating his character and example. And they must be accepted in the order in which the Saviour has placed them. A reversal of the order is fatal. If the sinner attempts to come *after* the Saviour before he has come *to* him, to copy the Redeemer's life and conduct without seeking peace with God by trust in the Redeemer's offering for sin, it will be an utter failure. A pacified conscience and a sense of being forgiven, must go before all true obedience. If, again, the sinner separates these two invitations, the consequence is equally fatal. If he attempts to obey the first without obeying the second, to come *to* Christ without coming *after* him, he is St. James's antinomian and his faith is dead faith without works. And if he attempts to obey the second invitation without obeying the first, to come *after* Christ without coming *to* him, he is St. Paul's legalist, who has no true sense of sin, rejects Christ's expiation, and expects salvation by moral character and a moral life.

VICARIOUS ATONEMENT AND PHILAN-
THROPY

"THE history of Islamism has ever been a history of crime, and to Christian morality alone do we owe all the social good that we enjoy." This is the judgment of Schweinfurth, the traveller who explored that part of Africa where the Mohammedan slave-dealers carry on their desolating trade. The remark is made after reciting a dreadful act of cruelty which passed under his own eyes. An emaciated and dying slave was dragged out of the hut into the broad and fierce light of the tropic sun, and there lashed with whips to prove whether life was yet extinct. The long white stripes upon the withered skin, and the writhing of the limbs, showed that soul and body were not yet separated. The cruelty continued until there were no signs of vitality, and then the slave-boys of the slave-dealer played at football with the corpse.

There are two doctrines taught in Christianity, and not taught in Mohammedanism, which if they were to become practical and operative in Africa, as they are in Europe, would utterly prevent such a scene as this. The first is that the incarnate Creator of mankind suffered and died for both the slave and the master, that their sins might be forgiven them. And the second is that every man ought to love his neighbor as himself. No cruelty can be practised when man acknowledges that all men are alike guilty beings before God, and that God has had such compassion upon them all as to give his only begotten Son to expiate their guilt. And no cruelty, of course, can be wrought by one who is animated by the philanthropy of the gospel. No man, says St. Paul in another connection, ever yet hated his own flesh; and no man who sees another self, as it were, in his fellow-man, can hate or harm him.

The doctrine of God's vicarious atonement is the root of all genuine and deep love between man and man. They who feel that they have been redeemed by a common blood and sacrifice, cannot bite or devour one another. This is the one touch of *grace*, that makes the whole world kin. There is no true and abiding source of good will among men, but the antecedent good will of God towards men. To tell a moral and reputable citizen of a Christian nation, who yet rejects the evangelical system, that he is capable of the same cruelty towards a fellow-man which Schweinfurth witnessed, would not only startle but anger him. He would say, "Is thy servant a dog, that he should do this thing?" And yet, so long as he does not really and affectionately love his fellow-man with a tender and gentle emotion, so long as grace has not overcome the innate selfishness of the human heart, he is as likely as any other man to act like the Mohammedan slave-dealer, under similar circumstances and temptations, and not restrained by the decencies of civilized life. And still more, if he lacks that particular and mighty motive of action which St. Paul alludes to when he pleads with his converts to "be gentle unto all men" in view of "the kindness and love of God our Saviour towards man," it is certain that in the heart of Africa, and in the situation of the Mohammedans, he would do as the Mohammedans do.

The evangelical doctrine of the atonement, while it implies the guilt and ruin of man, also implies the dignity of man. It is a humbling doctrine, but it is also an exalting one. This is too often overlooked. If man is a creature for whom the infinite and adorable God is willing to conceive and execute a method of mercy that involves the humiliation and suffering of one of the divine persons in the Godhead, surely man must be vastly above the brute in the scale of existence, and only a little lower than the angels. In the current discussion whether man sprung from the sea-slime, and is of the same nature with the ape, we have not observed that this argument has been urged. It cannot be that the Son of God would have left the eternal throne to redeem a mere animal. Unless man is made in the divine image, and is thereby different in kind from all the lower creation, he would not be the object of such an interest as is manifested in the work of Jesus Christ. If there were reasons which we do not understand why the eternal Son of God took not on him the nature of angels and did not redeem them, there are certainly reasons which we can well comprehend why he took not on him the nature of beasts and creeping things.

According to the view taken of the origin and nature of man by the materialist, such an act as that described by Schweinfurth, loses much of its horror. If that negro slave is of the same species with the dog, and there is nothing in his constitution that is kindred to the Eternal Spirit, and especially if there be no Eternal Spirit, why should not our feeling regarding it be only like that with which we contemplate the corporeal suffering of a brute? Why do we shudder at it as an enormity? The truth is, that the practical theory of the Mohammedan slave-trader agrees with the speculative theory of the materialist. The latter denies that man has an immortal and spiritual nature, and the former puts this theory to use. No more conclusive proof of the utter falsity of the infidel physics could be found, than to apply it unsparingly to human intercourse. The law of the strongest would indeed result in the survival of the fittest. The poor feeble pagan would be made a football by the vigorous Mohammedan, the world over.

THE DOCTRINE OF IMMORTALITY

In the month of August, 1802, William Wordsworth stood by the seashore at Calais, and saw the evening star slowly sink upon the shores of England. As the glittering orb settled nearer and nearer to the horizon, all his love and loyalty for his native land was kindled, and he gave expression to his deep and passionate feeling in that noble sonnet—the first of the series dedicated to Liberty—which ends with these lines:

> "There! that dusky spot
> Beneath thee, that is England; there she lies.
> Blessings be on you both! one hope, one lot,
> One life, one glory! I with many a fear
> For my dear country, many heartfelt sighs,
> Among men who do not love her, linger here."

Ninety years ago these emotions swelled in that mind, under that sky, upon that memorable seacoast, and beneath the sound of those waters rolling evermore. What is its consciousness at this moment? The poet no longer stands beneath the material heavens, and no sights or sounds that pass through the avenues of flesh and blood affect his mind. Yet he is as distinctly conscious in 1892 as he was in 1802. He lives in a world as real as that of France, and is subject to an experience as positive and clear as that which dilated him on the margin of the English Channel. If it were permitted him to embody his present emotions in the language of earth, the product would be as beautiful and thoughtful as the poetry of his loftiest moods here in time.

Such is the right manner of thinking of the dead; but do we spontaneously and easily think in this way? Although the doctrine of immortality is a common truth, and the Christian especially professes to believe it, yet those who have left this world are looked upon as having lost something by their departure from it. "Poor man, he is dead." How often do these words, coming without thought from our lips, show that we find this life more real and desirable than the other. We are obliged to correct our estimate by an after-thought, and reason ourselves into the conviction that to die is gain. Our first thought is not our best one. It is only the sober second thought which takes the true view of eternity as compared with time, of the world of spirits as compared with the world of matter.

That the natural man should commit this error is not strange. He is absorbed in the interests of time and earth, and estimates everything by the five senses. He minds carnal things, and the eye of his soul is shut to things unseen and eternal. It is no wonder that for him the world beyond this is a dim and undiscovered country, and that the only real and desirable region for him is this solid ground underfoot and this blue sky overhead. When Ulysses seeks to cheer the ghost of Achilles, by reminding him of the glory he had acquired by his deeds on earth, he makes answer: "I would rather live on earth the hireling of a poor swain, than to be king of all the souls in Hades." But it is strange, and it betokens an imperfect spirituality, a remaining worldliness, when the Christian finds it so difficult to be touched and impressed by "the power of an endless life." Immortality for the believer in Christ ought to be so bright and glorious as to throw a splendid light over all the gloom and sorrow of earth. This was the effect of the doctrine upon the Early church. The resurrection of the Redeemer had made the truth real and vivid. The other world was not nearly so far from this as Ultima Thule was from Rome. When a fellow-Christian died, he slept, he rested in peace. He was not far from his fellow-disciples, and hence they remembered his death-day by a visit to his grave, as we remember a friend's birthday by a visit to his house. If the Church of the present possessed more of this feeling, it would be bolder and more courageous in the battle with sin and Satan, and less under the spell of the lust of the flesh, the lust of the eye, and the pride of life.

The Spirit of God employs various means to produce this unearthly temper in the souls of his people. Sometimes a dangerous sickness brings eternity very near, and makes this world as unreal as a dream, and the other world as real as the solid ground. Trials, losses, sorrows, and all the discipline of life, are used as instruments to this same end by the gracious Comforter. We can co-work with him by turning our reflections toward the world whither we are rapidly going. It is good to remember that the principal feature in human existence anywhere, be it in this world or in another, is *consciousness*. If a man thinks and feels, this is the main thing about him. Whether he does it in the body or out of the body is a secondary matter, as it was in the instance when St. Paul was caught up to the third heavens and heard unspeakable things. Thought and feeling in the soul are no more necessarily confined to a particular kind of body, than they are to a particular style of clothes. The believer will not have his resurrection body, like that of the glorified Redeemer, until the day of judgment; but it does not follow from this that he will have no consciousness in his disembodied spirit between death and the resurrection. Consciousness accompanies the spirit everywhere, and flows right on from time over into eternity, without a break. The peace and joy of the dying believer, to which he gives faint utterance in his expiring words, do not become extinct by his soul's leaving the body and passing away from earth. The shining stream of consciousness sinks out of the sight of those who remain here, only to reappear in greater brilliancy as it pours itself into the sunlit sea beyond.

THE CERTAINTY OF FUTURE BLESSEDNESS

In no respect is the superiority of the Christian religion over all other religions more apparent, than in the manner in which it prepares man for death. We will not compare it with the lower, but the higher and better paganism in proof. The death of Socrates, as described by Plato, is the finest example of a placid departure from time into eternity, which the annals of man outside of revelation afford. Let us contemplate it, and see how much it implies, and then contrast it with the death of a believer in Christ. In the *Apology*, Socrates is represented as speaking as follows: "To be afraid of death, O Athenians, is in fact nothing else than to seem to be wise when a man is not wise: for it is to seem to have a knowledge of things which a man does not know. For no man really knows whether death may not be to mortal men of all blessings perhaps the greatest; and yet they do fear it as if they knew that it is the greatest of evils. And how, I ask, can this be other than the most shameful folly, to imagine that a man knows what he does not know?" To appeal to the ignorance of man, is not to construct a strong argument. To say to him, "You do not know with certainty whether you shall experience pain or pleasure in the future world; it may be, for aught you can tell, everlasting joy: why then do you fear?"—to meet his anxiety about the endless life hereafter with no better reasoning than this, is to excite his fears rather than to quell them. The interests at stake are so immense, that the mind cannot be satisfied with such a peradventure. Rabelais described his own religion as "a great perhaps." Such a happy immortality as this is "a great perhaps," and is poorly fitted to give the uneasy and apprehensive human soul the solace which it seeks when it thinks of the long existence which it is destined to live in the ages of eternity.

But in this argument of Socrates, no account is taken of the fears that arise from a sense of *guilt*. Perhaps this argument from the ignorance of man respecting the future might have some force for one who was innocent, or was conscious of having done good in this life. Indeed, Socrates evidently supposes that this is the case. He says that he has "had the best reason to believe that a god ordered him to spend his life in philosophizing, and in showing men how to live according to right reason." If now, he continues, he had, from fear of death, or from any other motive, left his post and disobeyed the god, this would have been a sin. And in this case he might well fear to die. But having obeyed the divine voice, he does not shrink from death, because it may bring a great joy instead of a great sorrow as most men fear it does. This reasoning implies a sense of innocence and righteousness upon the part of Socrates. How well founded and of what nature, we need not discuss here. But suppose a man is not possessed of this feeling, but, on the contrary, is conscious of having transgressed the moral law, and is feeling the sting of guilt? Then this argument, drawn from ignorance of what is in the future world, becomes utterly worthless. To the statement, "You know not what the future contains, and therefore it may bring to you endless pleasure," the guilt-smitten spirit replies, "I am a transgressor of the divine law, and I fear the retributions of the future."

But the truth is that the fear of death cannot be argued away by any method. Reasoning, good or bad, valid or weak, cannot give rest to the soul respecting this solemn subject of immortality. Nothing but a direct and immediate *consciousness* of peace with God and acceptance with him can do this. And here the gospel shows its power. "I know whom I have believed, and I am persuaded that he is able to keep that which I have committed unto him against that day. I am now ready to be offered, and the time of my departure is at hand. I have fought a good fight, I have finished my course, I have kept the faith. Henceforth there is laid up for me a crown of righteousness." St. Paul, when he wrote these words, had the same kind of evidence for a blessed immortality that he had for his own existence. It was the evidence of consciousness. No man can prove his own existence by a syllogistical argument, because the premises of such an argument must be more certain than the conclusion, and no one can be more certain of anything than he is that he exists. And for the same reason a syllogistical argument in disproof of one's own existence cannot be constructed. Now, a believer in Christ is possessed of an experience in regard to the future world which has the same kind of force. He cannot construct a proof that he shall enjoy a blessed life beyond the grave which will have the force of a mathematical proof, and neither can such a kind of argument be constructed as evidence against a happy immortality. Hence all the reasonings of Socrates and Plato upon this subject, although they favor the doctrine and go to render its truthfulness probable, cannot make it absolutely certain. Only that religion which is able to *produce a consciousness* in the soul itself, is competent to produce certainty. And this is done by the gospel of Christ. A believer's confidence of happiness hereafter springs out of his religious experience, and not out of his ratiocinations. When the divine life which Christ imparts is active, the disciple has a hope full of immortality. But when it wanes, doubts and fears come in.

The secret, therefore, of an assured belief in a blessed future life, is an exalted and vigorous religious experience. Since the whole force of the evidence for it consists in the person's consciousness, it is necessary to have this consciousness. There must be a "taste of the heavenly gift," a sense of "the power of an endless life." But a taste, a sense, an experimental feeling is a gift of God. No man can give himself a consciousness of any kind. This is always a Divine product. A man's consciousness of his own existence is the work of his Maker. It is no arrangement or provision of the man himself. And still more is it true that the consciousness of a believer is the product of God working in the soul. No man can fill himself with such a feeling as that which swelled the heart of St. Paul when he said, "I know whom I have believed." It comes only when the Holy Ghost sheds abroad the love of God in the heart. He then who would become independent of all arguments, either for or against a blessed immortality, and would have a direct and unassailable conviction of the truth, must "walk in the Spirit," and thus "not fulfil the desires of the flesh."

THE HABIT OF READING THE BIBLE

The diary of the late John Quincy Adams affords interesting glimpses of the private life of a distinguished politician for upwards of a half century. The seventh volume allows us to enter the White House and see how a President of the United States spent his time, and discharged his duties, sixty years ago. Among other things, we learn that it was his habit in the summer season, to swim for an hour or so in the Potomac, before sunrise, and that in one instance when he attempted to swim across the river he narrowly escaped losing his life by drowning.

But the most interesting feature in President Adams's life is exhibited in the following extract from the diary—a diary, it should be remembered, which was written with the utmost freedom and intended to be seen by no eye but his own, and which has been sifted before publication of much which it would be improper to disclose to the world. The second Adams was a man of strong political prejudices, and undoubtedly expressed his mind without reserve respecting political men, parties, and measures, but under the admirable supervision of his son, Charles Francis Adams, nothing appears that could wound the feelings of any.

The extract is this: " I rise usually between five and six—that is, at this time of the year, from an hour and a half to two hours before the sun. I walk by the light of the moon or stars, or none, about four miles, usually returning home in time to see the sun rise from the eastern chamber of the house. I then make my fire, and *read three chapters in the Bible, with Scott's and Hewlet's Commentaries.*" There are some points that are noticeable in respect to the passage which we have italicized. In the first place, the writer was not a Calvinist in his theological belief, yet he seeks to understand the Word of God by the aid of that plain and cogent interpreter who was the trusted friend of John Newton and William Cowper, and whose commentaries, though now somewhat displaced by others, yet contributed as much as any other uninspired production to the spread of evangelical religion in Great Britain and America. In his theological opinions, the second Adams seems to have been an Arian in regard to the divinity of Christ, and an opponent of the doctrine of vicarious atonement. But his early religious education, together with a sense of accountability to God which he carried with him continually, and which led him to take a solemn view of human life here below, made him not unwilling to read his Bible by the light of a commentator with whom upon some important subjects he had little sympathy, but with whose opinions respecting the more general aspects of morality and religion he found himself agreeing. The earlier form of Unitarianism which is represented by such men as Adams, retained many of the serious and solemn elements of that orthodox faith from which it had departed not abruptly but gradually. The belief in the inspiration and authority of the Scriptures, in the miraculous conception though not divine nature of Jesus Christ, and in a state of future rewards and punishments, led men of this stamp to read their Bible, to keep the Sabbath, and to strive to live an upright and moral life. It is to be feared that at the present time there are many political men whose theological creed is nearer to the teaching of Scripture than was that of John Quincy Adams, who yet do not rise early in the morning to read three chapters of the Bible with the help of Scott's Commentary.

And this leads us to notice a second point regarding this extract from the diary. It is that this politician and statesman of an elder day went to the Scriptures for all his information upon the subject of religion. He believed that if the secret of human destiny cannot be cleared up by the Bible, it cannot be cleared up at all. The thought of going to the Vedas, or to the writings of Confucius or Sakyamuni, for information by which to be guided through this world into another, would have seemed to him to be the height of absurdity. The difference between the earlier and later Socinianism of New England in this respect is very great. The fathers when they wanted religion betook themselves to the Scriptures of the Christian Church; the children, some of them, at least, betake themselves to the sacred books of India and China.

There is no habit of more real value to any man, be he public or private, than this of the sixth President of the United States. It is to be feared that partly on account of the excessive multiplication of religious books, even those who have been religiously educated do not maintain the habit with the regularity and pertinacity of an earlier generation. He who can take down the English Bible and read consecutively three chapters, and find intellectual stimulus, to say nothing of moral and spiritual edification, in so doing, thereby evinces that he has a robust understanding. This is one secret of that good, hard sense, that downright honesty, that bold integrity bordering sometimes upon bluntness, which are seen in the statesmen of the honest and the heroic age in our national history.

A LITTLE RELIGION IS A DANGEROUS THING

"A little learning," says Bacon, "is a dangerous thing." So likewise is a little religion. If it be good advice to a student to bid him drink deep or taste not the fountain of science, it is equally good advice to a man to bid him be thorough in religion, or else let it alone. Our Lord so instructs, when he says, " Either make the tree good and his fruit good, or else make the tree corrupt, and his fruit corrupt." What then are some of the dangers of a little religion? They are both speculative and practical.

A superficial religion raises difficult questions, but does not furnish their answers. There is just knowledge enough to cause the person to perceive the objections to the doctrines of Christianity, but not sufficient experience of the power of these doctrines in the heart to silence them. Take for illustration the doctrine of atonement. He whose faith in Christ's blood is weak, because his sense of sin is slight, will be the subject of painful doubts, at times, respecting the reality and reasonableness of this cardinal truth. Had he a profound and unwavering confidence in Christ, he would be able to quell these suspicions concerning this part of divine revelation. There is no answer to a sceptical doubt equal to an immediate consciousness; but no one can have this upon any subject if he is superficial. Consciousness is a personal sense and feeling, and it is impossible for a sceptic to gain ground when this is in his way. If a man's belief in the atonement is mainly the result of reasoning, if he holds this tenet chiefly by dint of argument, there will be times when his faith will waver; and if there be nothing more than this to steady it, in the end he will fail to retain his hold. But if, like St. Paul, he can say, "I know whom I have believed, and I am persuaded that he is able to keep that which I have committed unto him against that day," like the great apostle, he will be proof against all the wiles of error and infidelity. St. Paul endured many temptations, but there is nothing in all his writings that suggests in the least the thought that possibly he may have been the subject of sceptical doubts. John the Baptist wavered and queried, and sent two of his disciples, saying, "Art thou he that should come, or do we look for another?" But St. Paul, from the day that he saw Christ on the way to Damascus, never doubted for a moment that he was the eternal Redeemer.

It is the remark of Augustine, if we mistake not, that there is no more dangerous period in the history of the Church than that in which questions are raised, but are not answered. If this be true, we are now living in a dangerous time. The capacity for doubt is greater than the capacity for removing doubt. And if any one is hasty to conclude that this is a sign of great intellectual ability, let him remember the homely proverb that "any fool can ask a question, but only a wise man can answer it." The infidelity which filters through the community so extensively arises very much from a superficial apprehension. The doubt whether prayer is efficacious is started by the objection that God is immutable, or that the Divine Being cannot be supposed to concern himself with the interests of a single individual. But these objections would have no force for a mind that took a deeper view of the divine immutability, and saw that immutability does not mean insensibility; or that perceived that for the Divine infinitude there is nothing great or small, but that all things alike being the creatures of God are alike the objects of his providential care. Neither would they have force for one who was in the habit of daily fervent prayer. He who pours out his soul to God, and finds spiritual refreshment and evident answers to his petitions in his personal experience, cannot be shaken by infidel objections. There may be some aspects of the subject which are mysterious to him, and there may be some questions which he cannot answer, but he will not permit the unknown to nullify the known. "Whether he be a sinner or no, I know not. One thing I know, that whereas I was blind now I see." This was good reasoning. No man can surrender his belief in facts of personal experience, however dim or uncertain may be his knowledge of the remote and hidden causes of these facts.

The age needs, therefore, two things: first, a deeper religious knowledge, and, second, a deeper religious experience. The two go together. It is interesting to observe how free from all morbid experiences and distressing doubts have been all the strong and earnest minds in Christian history. Luther and Calvin give no signs of the tremor of unbelief. They held the doctrines of Christianity in what would be denominated their severest and most difficult form. The doctrines of original sin and predestination are better calculated than almost any others to baffle explanation, and to engender scepticism. But these doctrines enter thoroughly into the Early Lutheran and Calvinistic schemes. They are not softened down from the Scripture representation, but are presented in their sharpness. Yet neither of these Reformers staggers in unbelief; and what is yet more, they never appear to feel any difficulties. In this respect, they are like their Lord and Master, who, after saying that he goes to death in the way that is predetermined, immediately adds, that the human instrument by which the Divine decree is fulfilled is so free and so guilty that it would have been better for him if he had never been born.

NOT WEALTH, BUT COMPETENCE

THE present generation of Christians is too busy to be highly religious. In order to deep piety, there must be leisure for reading God's Word and religious books, and opportunity for reflection upon divine things. The mind cannot do two things at once. If a Christian is engaged from morning to night solely in the prosecution of business, it is impossible that he should bring his heart into contact with things unseen and eternal; and without such a contact his piety must be feeble and faint. But the present mode of living, especially in large cities, is such that all classes are driven by worldly occupations, and no time is left for higher and better reflections. The last generation of merchants were more favorably situated than the present, for the cultivation of the soul. Fifty years ago the merchant lived near his place of business, took his meals with his family, spent his evenings in his own home, and enjoyed the privileges of his church and the intercourse of a sober-minded and thoughtful circle of friends and neighbors. He had leisure for meditation upon his soul and its needs. The consequence was, that he was a more devout person than his successor. The churches of the last generation were blessed with revivals of religion, and religion penetrated all classes of society more generally than it now does.

How then can the evil be remedied? How shall the disciple of Christ gain time for the study of God's Word and for private devotion? By retrenching his business. Good men are laying too broad plans for the acquisition of wealth. They have set their aim too high. The amount of money which they deem necessary for their families is far too great. Here is the root of the evil that ramifies so widely. The Christian father of a family has put hundreds of thousands where he should have put tens, and thousands where he should have put hundreds, in his estimate of the property which he ought to accumulate. Any careful reader of the Bible will see that *competency*, and not wealth, is the goal that is set up for the church-member. He is commanded to provide for his family so that they may not be dependent and poor. Further than this, he is not commanded and he is not permitted to go. Agur's prayer is the prayer for him: "Give me neither poverty nor riches." They that desire to be rich fall into many hurtful snares that drown men in perdition. The love of money is the root of much of the evil that is now afflicting the Church of Christ.

Suppose that the present generation of Christian merchants should substitute independence for wealth, in their estimate of what their business life should bring them—what would be the result? The immediate consequence would be, more repose of mind and more leisure. The great strain which is knocking down so many men with apoplexy and paralysis at the age of fifty, would be taken off. A man can acquire a competency without any convulsive effort. But to become a millionaire, he must make spasmodic endeavors. Prudence, industry, and economy, with the Divine blessing (and the Divine blessing travels this road), will render any man independent in his circumstances. But these are qualities that do not so absorb all the time and energy as to leave no remainder for other objects and aims. The daily life of an independent man, who lives within his means, and intends that his children shall do the same after him, is a noble and honorable one. It has nothing of the meanness and vulgarity of the devotee of wealth and fashion. There is no struggle either to be or to appear rich, but the calm and self-possessed bearing of one who owes no man anything but to love one another. Some one remarks that "equality, in the cant of politics, means the wish to be equal to one's superiors, and to be superior to one's equals." This is also the spirit of the purse-proud. It is not the spirit of a true republican, a true gentleman, or a true Christian.

It is the first step that costs. And in bringing about a change in the church, or in a church-member, the first thing is also the most difficult— viz.: to determine to accept competence in lieu of wealth. The moment the disciple of Christ has resolved in the strength of Christ not to become rich, but only to become independent in his circumstances, the hardest part of the work is done. It is the large wealth that is in the dim distance, that is luring on the professed disciple of him who had not where to lay his head. If instead of the hundreds of thousands, he would substitute the tens of thousands, he would find his life more even tempered, more happy, and more useful. Should Christ appear on earth and speak the word most needed in the present juncture, it would be the words which he addressed to Martha: "Thou art troubled about many things."

DENOMINATIONAL UNITY UNDESIRABLE

Evangelical Christendom is composed of Christians whose creed is either that of Calvin or that of Arminius. Those persons who cannot adopt the fundamental views of one or the other of these theological leaders, must be counted out. They are not "evangelical," because they reject the doctrine of Christ's divinity and of forgiveness through his atonement—doctrines common to all Trinitarians. The various evangelical denominations, therefore, though some of them do not adopt everything in Calvinism, and others of them not everything in Arminianism, are yet fairly enough ranged under these two types of theology. In some churches, as the Episcopalian, for example, both in Great Britain and America, both forms of doctrine are tolerated, though both forms are not contained in the Thirty-nine Articles. In others, as the Methodist, pure and simple Arminianism is the ruling faith; in others, as the Presbyterian and the Reformed, pure and simple Calvinism has been the creed and the experience of the general membership. Go through evangelical

Christendom and examine the religious experience of every man who hopes to be saved by the blood and righteousness of Christ, and it will be found to have either the Calvinistic or the Arminian shape and tinge. The individual himself may not be aware of the tinge, but it is there, produced by the religious education which he has received from his parents, and the ministry of the Church to which he belongs.

Would it be for the interest of Christ's kingdom here upon earth, to unite all these evangelical denominations into a single body? Would it speed the progress of the gospel through this sinful world, to bring Arminians and Calvinists together in a single denomination? We say No, and will mention a reason. It is not the only reason, but it is a strong one. It would be impossible *to educate and license a ministry* for such a complex denomination. The power of a religious body, so far as human agency is concerned, depends upon its religious teachers. Hence, the most important part of a church's work consists in training its clergy. All the rest of the work of a denomination, in planting churches at home and abroad, and caring for them, will be an utter failure if its ministry is uneducated and weak. Each and every ecclesiastical denomination consequently takes special pains, by institutions, faculties of instruction, and large endowments, to provide for ministerial education. But supposing a union of Calvinists and Arminians, what shall be the system of doctrine taught in its theological schools?

Who shall be appointed to deliver lectures in divinity to the classes? If Arminianism were selected, it would be impossible for conscientious and earnest Calvinists to acquiesce in this arrangement. If Calvinism were selected, it would be equally impossible for conscientious and earnest Arminians to be satisfied. There would be conflict in the new denomination immediately regarding that one subject, the training of ministers, which more than any other is fitted to agitate a religious organization to the inmost. But some ingenious person may suggest that a compromise creed might be manufactured—a compound of the two systems. This is an impossibility. Arminianism and Calvinism, though having an evangelical substratum in common, both alike "holding the head"—namely, that Christ is God, and that his blood is the only atonement for sin—yet differ upon certain subjects connected with these vital truths, in such a clear and decided manner that the only union between them must be by transubstantiation. The one must convert the other, or the other must convert the one. The mixture of both is bad. We are Calvinists, but we do not hesitate to say that Arminianism, pure and simple, frank and manly, is far preferable to Calvinism modified by Arminian elements. And we doubt not that an intelligent Arminian would say that outspoken and unequivocal Calvinism, is much better than Arminianism dashed with the bitter bowls of decrees and predestination. And the reason is, that there is *honesty* upon both sides when the pure and simple system, without attempt at admixture, is presented. Honest and open-minded men respect each other, while they differ, and in their differences. But in all attempts to mix the immiscible, there must be more or less of management, finesse, and intrigue. Insincerity and hypocrisy, unconsciously, if not intentionally, creep in. One party strives to outwit the other, and the result is a quarrelsome married life, ending in a divorce.

It is plain that to unite evangelical denominations having such settled and distinct doctrinal differences as the Methodists and Presbyterians, for example, would be the destruction of theological education in the united body. They could not educate a clergy; and they could not license them, if they could have them educated outside of the denomination. Imagine a candidate for the ministry appearing before an ecclesiastical body composed about equally of conscientious adherents of Wesley and Calvin! The answers satisfactory to one division must be unsatisfactory to the other; and the young minister could not go forth with the cordial approbation and support of the entire body.

But while organic and ecclesiastical union between the Arminian and Calvinistic worlds is both impossible and undesirable, the moral and spiritual union, which is grounded in a common trust in the Divine Redeemer and his atoning blood, is both possible and actual. There is, to-day, a better understanding between the pious Methodist and the pious Presbyterian, and a more hearty and generous love for each other as brethren in the Lord, as they now are, in two denominations, than there would be if they were in one. Two families, each living in its own house, have more affection and less friction than two families living under one roof. And the reason is, that, by this arrangement, the peculiarities and preferences of one family do not clash with those of the other. Each sees the good qualities of the other, while the disagreeable traits of each are not observed. And this would be equally true if the supposed families were blood relations. So is it with the different branches of Christ's household. Within the province of practical life and experience, there is union and harmony among all of Christ's true disciples. The prayer-meeting, benevolent work, and social intercourse elicit a common feeling, and all evangelical denominations flow together. But within the province of theory and systematic instruction, the disciples of Christ do not yet all see eye to eye, and it is within this province that conflict and collision arise. Hence, it is best that an ecclesiastical union should not be brought about between those who know that they have these differences. For an ecclesiastical organization, unlike a union conference in a common benevolent enterprise, brings into view the speculative aspects of religion; the whole great subject of the ministry, and the creed which the ministry shall preach. But the acts of public worship and of coöperation in missionary labors, relate only to the practical aspects of religion, and respecting these the great mass of communicants, the brotherhood at large, in all the evangelical churches, can and do mingle with each other in fraternal love and confidence. Even their suspicions are more amusing than serious. A pious old lady, of the Calvinistic faith, remarked concerning her son who had joined the Methodist Church: "He is as good a son as ever lived, but I hate him, he is such an Arminian." Such "hatred" as this would not prove to be a very serious bar to communion between the Christian mother and the Christian son. It is a very different thing from the *odium theologicum*, which is much more certain to arise between opposing parties in one ecclesiastical denomination, than between two distinct and strong denominations each respecting the other, and each doing its appointed work until the time arrive when there "shall be one flock and one shepherd."

The recent attempt to introduce an alien and anti-Calvinistic theology into the Northern Presbyterian Church, strongly illustrates the divisive nature of a dual theology in a single denomination. The plain antagonism between the doctrine of the Briggs Inaugural and that of the Westminster Standards was immediately perceived by the great mass of the denomination, and the former was condemned as heresy by an overwhelming majority. To permit its inculcation in the theological seminaries, and its spread amongst the ministry, was seen to be suicidal. The unanimity of the Church in its decision to adhere to its ancestral faith, made this attempt of a party to effect a departure from it comparatively harmless. But had the "liberal theology" proved to have been the doctrine of half of the body, there would have been a division into two denominations. As the case now stands, the number of malcontents will probably diminish, and those who upon the second sober thought cannot sincerely adopt the public sentiment of the Church will seek other ecclesiastical connections, if they are honorable and self-respecting. But even a division of the denomination would be better for both parties, than the continuance of both under one organization with an internecine conflict in creed and measures.

AN AMERICAN FAULT

The people of the United States, to a spectator, are *political* in their tendency. They are agitated by the ballot more than by anything else. They choose a president once in every four years, and the interval between is filled up with scores of elections, from that of governor to constable. Irving, in one of his humorous papers, speaking of the Frenchman's propensity for dancing, calculates that the Frenchman, owing to this custom, spends at least one-fourth of his time in the air. By a similar calculation, it might perhaps be found that an American citizen spends a tenth of his time in electing officers.

It is a good thing for a nation, as it is for an individual, to confess its faults. The most unfavorable symptom in the case of the American, is his unwillingness to acknowledge that the people to whom he belongs have any defects. He is quick to discover the evils of monarchy and aristocracy, but he is blind to those of democracy. And among these latter evils that of excessive devotion to the business of self-government is perhaps the greatest.

In the first place, it leads to a false estimate of politics itself, as compared with other subjects. Would it be rash to say that the majority of the American people prefer political distinction to distinction in letters, art, science, and religion? Go through the country and ask the aspiring young man which he would prefer to be, president of the United States, or author of *Paradise Lost*, and in four instances out of five the answer would be: president of the United States. Try him by a similar inquiry respecting the relative importance of politics and fine art, politics and science, and politics and religion, and a similar reply would be given. Those who have young men under their care are struck with this strange propensity to over-estimate an inferior department like politics, and under-estimate a superior one like literature. The college professor often sees a youth of fine talents and opportunities turning away from "the high-erected thoughts and planet-like music" of Plato and Shakespeare, and descending to the low level of a partisan newspaper and a partisan legislature, for the arena in which to work his mind and employ his collegiate training.

Now, this estimate is utterly false. Political reputation and influence, compared with literary, are ephemeral. In the days of Queen Elizabeth, the great name in English politics was that of Lord Burleigh; and his name was in every mouth. Contemporary with him there was a writer of plays whose name was then unknown out of a narrow circle connected with the theatre. His name was William Shakespeare. Who hears now of Burleigh, or has heard of him for two centuries? But even the most unlettered of politicians has heard of Shakespeare. Compare the present and future influence and reputation of Robert Peel and William Wordsworth; of Gladstone and Tennyson; of Thomas Jefferson and Jonathan Edwards; and it is easy to see that devotion to politics is a waste of mental power, in comparison with devotion to letters and religion.

And the reason is this: government is nowadays concerned with merely the person and the property. It cares for the earthly and secular interests of mankind. Whoever, therefore, devotes himself to this subject exclusively and alone, is busied with inferior affairs alone. He is looking after the farm and the merchandise; and unless he can bring into his politics something from a higher quarter, he will be like Bunyan's man with a muckrake who never looks up into the sky, but continually looks down into the dirt in which he is raking. When the young man who has received a liberal education turns the whole native force and all the acquired discipline of his intellect to the discussion of such themes as tariffs, patent-rights, banking, trade, manufactures, and the like, he is really descending into a province only one step above that of the day-laborer and artisan. There is nothing in such subjects that is fitted to elevate or widen his mind. And still more, if he bends all his power to the furtherance of merely partisan designs, if he absorbs all his energy in the mere arts of a demagogue, does he waste and degrade his intellect. We know that the old Greek idea of politics made it something nobler than this. But it was because that under the Grecian constitutions the interests of religion and learning were identified with those of government. But under the democratical constitution of the United States, owing to the jealousy of contending sects and the fear that learning is aristocratic, religion and letters are divorced from politics, so that nothing is left to government but the management of purely material interests. Hence, instead of the ancient statesman, we have the modern politician. The political arena is no longer graced by the presence of men of comprehensive knowledge and finished education. The Everetts and Legares have long ago ceased to go to Congress.

A second evil of this extreme inclination to political life in the American people, is the decline of letters and religion. The mental energy being absorbed in the struggle to attain office and to keep it when attained, nothing is left that can be applied to higher themes. There is no surer way to deaden a young man's interest in the elegant ideas of literature, or the solemn ideas of religion, than to nominate him as a candidate for political honors, and run him in the race for them. The taste begins to grow vulgar, the instant the still air of delightful studies is deserted for the foul air of the caucus and the popular assembly. This process is going on continually, and one needs only open his eyes to see it. Political circles, as they appear at the state and national capitals, with some few exceptions, are composed of persons upon whom a finished essay in letters, or a profound lecture in morals, would be wasted and lost. They are not in the mood for such discourse. And whoever joins these circles and remains in them imbibes the same spirit. He may have come from the refined and thoughtful society which is still to be found in those portions of the land where the institutions of religion and learning exert their elevating influence, and may resolve in his own mind to carry his religion and his literature into politics; but the current proves to be too strong for him, and he must either get out of it or be carried along with it.

What shall be done in the case? it will be asked. The ministry have a duty; and this is to rectify the public opinion upon this subject. Let them instil into the minds of the young men the old doctrine, that no vocation is so honorable as that of a clergyman or teacher; that next to this stands the lawyer and physician; and that next to these professions stands some legitimate and useful occupation or business. When this shall once more be the public opinion, as it was in the earlier and better era in our history, then the professions and the ranks of business men will once more be filled up with educated and upright citizens, from whom the officers of government will be chosen, not because they wish for office, but because they are fit for office, and the people desire them to be their rulers.

POLITICAL FANATICISM

The dictionary defines a fanatic to be "a religious enthusiast; a visionary; one who indulges wild and extravagant notions of religion." It does not seem to have occurred to the lexicographer that fanaticism may exist in other provinces than that of religion, and that wild and extravagant notions may be indulged respecting temporal as well as eternal things. Religion is not the only subject that may be abused by the visionary and enthusiast. There is fanaticism in trade and business. The stock market often presents this appearance. The brokers' board is sometimes a rabble of wild fanatics. No excesses of a negro camp-meeting are greater than those which are sometimes witnessed in Broad Street or the Paris Bourse. Men have died from excitement about money, as they have from excitement about religion. Constitutions have been shattered by the strain upon the nerves caused by the fear of losing wealth, as they have been by the strain produced by the fear of hell.

There is fanaticism in politics also, and to this

we would direct attention for a moment. We do not by any means deny that government is of great importance, and that a proper degree of interest in its administration is a duty. Patriotism, though not piety, any more than family affection is holiness, is an instinctive feeling implanted by the Creator that is amiable and attractive. It belongs to man's constitution, and is to be cultivated and especially to be sanctified. But one chief mode of cultivating and sanctifying the sentiment is to *moderate* it. If it be allowed to become rampant and drive out other and higher sentiments and subjects, then patriotism becomes fanaticism, and this fanaticism is wrong. Its utterance is: "My country right or wrong; my party right or wrong." The claims of a man's country are inferior to the claims of God upon him. Politics is second to religion. Hence if a man devote his time, his strength, and his thoughts so excessively to the political party to which he belongs as to neglect the concerns of his own soul and the religious welfare of his family and society, then his so-called patriotism is a sin.

Now, looking over the field of American politics we think that any candid observer must say that there is much political fanaticism in the American people. The annual elections in the several States, or in the country at large, excite the population unduly and extravagantly. There is no reason in the state of the case for such an excitement every twelve months. If it were a great crisis in the history of the people, such as that of the late war, imperilling the existence of the government, there would be more excuse for such an absorption in politics. But the questions that arise in a time of peace at an annual election, relate only to secondary matters which are not vital to the existence of the American Union. What man in his senses believes that if the party favoring specie payment gets the rule, the American Republic will really and actually be broken up and cease to be one of the nations of the earth? And what sane man will assert that if the party of inflation obtains power, the experiment of self-government will have proved to be a failure in the United States? More or less of specie, more or less of paper money, are not the things that decide the destiny of this republic. The same questions might be put respecting the tariff. Is it impossible for the nation to live under a high tariff? Must it of necessity die under a low one? And yet the great mass of the American people, in an election, act as if these matters of money and temporal prosperity were of more consequence than all others, and as if one policy or the other were the only possible and allowable policy. Politics differs from religion in this particular, namely, that several ways may be allowed, and if a mistake is made it can be corrected. Government is an uncertain and experimental science. It is often difficult to say which is the better of two propositions, or two measures. Nothing but the trial will decide. Men may therefore properly differ in politics. But religion is fixed in its principles and methods, and men may not properly differ in religion. There is only one name given under heaven among men whereby they must be saved. Religion is not an uncertain and experimental science. It is drawn out in black and white in a written volume. If a mistake is made in religion, it cannot be corrected. A man may be whig or tory, republican or democrat, and be a truly good man in the sight of God. But a man cannot be christian or infidel, a believer in Christ or a rejecter of Christ, and be a truly good man in the sight of God.

The great defect in American politics is fanaticism. Let your moderation in politics be known to all men, is the true maxim for the people. It will be a happy day when the masses of our citizens shall be as greatly excited upon the subject of morals and religion as they now are upon politics, and as moderate in their political excitements as they now are in their religious.

THE DANGERS OF OFFICE-HOLDING

The motto upon the escutcheon of the Earl of Lonsdale is, *Magistratus indicat virum:* the magistracy shows the man. Office-holding is a test of character. He who can resist the temptations to injustice, fraud, deceit, and self-aggrandizement generally, which beset one who either inherits office or obtains it by the popular suffrage, is unquestionably a person of deep convictions of truth, and of high moral principle. For this reason, public life would not be sought by one who distrusts himself. He who puts up the petition, " Lead me not into temptation," would be thankful for the providence that should forever keep him in the quiet and independent walks of private life. Should the will of God oblige him to assume the responsibility of a judge, a magistrate, or a legislator, he would enter upon them, not because he preferred them, but because duty must be discharged toward God. It was in this spirit that the better class of public men, in the early and better era in American history, entered upon office. Washington, had his inclination been his guide, would not have accepted office. The people forced it upon him. And before he would have employed money to secure his election, before he would have even solicited a vote from a fellow-citizen, much as he loved his country, he would have seen it the prey of all manner of evil.

But this is not the present estimate of public office. Men do not shrink from it as calculated to put a great strain upon their morality and integrity, but they rush in crowds, and almost to a man, after its emoluments and honors. The people of the United States are a nation of office-seekers, as much as the English, according to Napoleon, were a nation of shopkeepers. No one stops to consider the risks to character and morals which he incurs by getting office, but strains every muscle to obtain what he thinks to be a prize. This spirit has been dominant for many years in the nation. It has increased with fearful rapidity during the last few years. It now threatens the destruction of the republic. Unless there be a change in this respect, democracy in America will go the way of all democracy in the past. Republics, in history, have been short-lived, and nothing but very decided integrity and moral purity can make the United States an exception to the general fact.

The dangers of office-holding in this country have now become so great that no one is fit to hold office who does not realize them. Show us a man who has no fears of the bribery, the immorality, the irreligion which prevail in the party caucus which now controls all nominations and decides all elections, and we will show you an American citizen who ought not to take office. The recent exposure at Washington of what has been going on in the dark for some time, shows that the instant a man leaves the privacy of his home and of the district to which he belongs, and goes to the national capital, he is assailed by temptation of the lowest and basest kind. Doubtless some of those who have fallen under these temptations were persons of some conscience and moral principle when they left private life for public position; while others were probably tainted at the start. But the movement was downward with both classes.

But what is the remedy for this state of things? The cure, if it come at all, must begin with a sense and acknowledgment of the disease. They that are whole need not a physician; and they who think and say that they are whole do not apply to a physician. All men are optimists, and none more so than Americans. There is an obstinate conviction in their minds that all will turn out well for republics and republican institutions. Aristocracies and monarchies are destined to destruction, but universal suffrage, like gravitation, will hold all things to the centre and keep them firm. Though there may be venality in State and national legislatures, and public officers may be fraudulent and vicious, yet the inherent vigor of popular government will in the end triumph over all those evils which have destroyed other governments. But this optimism will prove to be fatal. A strong and good government cannot be secured by merely throwing ballots into a box. The mere form of government is not sufficient to secure protection to life and property. The city of New York has a democratic form of government, pure and simple, and yet human life is less safe under it than it is in London or Berlin; and the recent robbery of the city treasury by the Tweed administration has reached to an amount unheard of in the history of the world. Those who refuse to take counsel of fear, and have no apprehension lest the experiment of self-government in the United States prove to be a failure, are taking the sure course to make it such. A wise and serious anxiety ought to be the temper of an American citizen in the present attitude and aspect of American politics. The stream cannot rise above its fountain-head. The ballot of universal suffrage cannot be any purer than the constituency that casts it. And if that constituency become, in the majority, ignorant, vicious, and godless, then the problem of self-government becomes insoluble. Democracy, in this case, is self-government with the *devil* for the self.

THE UNION AND THE WAR[1]

Psalm 118:6, 7. "The Lord is on my side; I will not fear: what can man do unto me? The Lord taketh my part with them that help me; therefore shall I see my desire upon them that hate me."

This is a portion of a psalm that was indited most probably by King David, to be sung upon a day of thanksgiving by the people of Israel, as they moved in solemn and jubilant procession to the temple of the Most High, to offer praise for a great national deliverance. We do not know the particular occasion, the precise victory, that inspired this sacred anthem. Some commentators think they find internal evidence that David could not have been its author, and that it was composed, on the return from the exile, for the dedication of the second temple. But there are many chapters in the life of the royal harper that were fitted to inspire such a psalm of deliverance; and it accords well with similar thanksgivings in the book of Psalms that are universally ascribed to his

[1] A Discourse delivered in the Brick Church, New York, November 27, 1862.

authorship. Be this as it may, it is an inspired lyric that expresses clearly and strongly the jubilance of the people of God when his arm has wrought deliverance for them; and in every age it has been an anthem through which they have uttered their praises when the right hand of the Lord was exalted, and when the right hand of the Lord did valiantly for his church. It is also a thanksgiving psalm for an individual, as well as a nation. Those heroes of the Christian church, those confessors, martyrs, and reformers who have been called to great sorrows and to great triumphs in their own personal experiences, have betaken themselves to this one hundred and eighteenth psalm as the trumpet through which they sounded out their glorying in the God that had helped them and had given them the victory. Martin Luther, we are told, appropriated this psalm for his peculiar comfort, and wrote the seventeenth verse of it ("I shall not die, but live and declare the works of the Lord") upon the walls of his study, saying, "This is my psalm which I love. Though I love all the psalms and the Scriptures, and regard them as the comfort of my life, yet I have had such experience of this psalm, that it must remain, and shall be called, *my* psalm; for it has been very precious to me, has delivered me out of many troubles, and without it neither emperor, kings, the wise and prudent, nor saints, could have helped me."

In reading this psalm, it will be observed that the strong and firm foundation upon which the rejoicing and the thanksgiving rest, is the fact *that God had been upon the side of the victors;* and this implies that truth and right were upon their side. David and the people of Israel did not rejoice merely because they had "quenched" the nations that had "compassed them about like bees," as a man quenches the flashy "fire of thorns." It was not the secular and vainglorious rejoicing of a warlike people over a great victory and a new conquest, without any regard to the right and wrong of the war, without any reference to the moral principles that were involved in the contest. It was no merely Roman triumph, stretching many a mile with spoils and captives, adding another province to the immense pagan despotism of the old world, and ministering afresh to the pride and glory of an earthly domination. It was a Jewish triumph, a theocratic victory, gained by the favor of Jehovah, founded in a righteous cause, and subserving the interests of that spiritual kingdom of which the Son of God and the Son of David is the Lord and King. The Roman general stood in a triumphal chariot, attired in a gold-embroidered robe, bearing in his right hand a laurel bough and in his left a sceptre, and his brows encircled with an oaken garland. He was the central figure in the pomp, and the few religious ceremonies that accompanied the procession, as it moved up to the capitol and "Jove's eternal fane," were all eclipsed and lost in the adulations offered to a mortal. But the king of Israel went on foot, with the priests and the people, clothed in the simple linen tunic, the girdle, and the mitre, and his utterance was: "O give thanks to the Lord, for he is good; for his mercy endureth forever. Let Israel now say that his mercy endureth forever. Let the house of Aaron now say that his mercy endureth forever. The Lord is on my side. The Lord taketh my part with them that help me. It is better to trust in the Lord than to put confidence in man. It is better to trust in the Lord than to put confidence in princes." It is the utterance not of a proud and self-conscious emperor but of a servant of the Most High, in meekness and thankfulness ascribing glory to him from whom all glories are.

We have selected this text because it naturally conducts us to a series of reflections that are appropriate to the circumstances in which we assemble at the call of our chief magistrate, to offer thanksgiving to God. For some of the circumstances are peculiar and sad. We are invited to be glad and thankful in the midst of the most melancholy and exhausting of wars, a civil war. Yet the invitation is a reasonable one. For there is no condition of man here upon earth in which he does not enjoy some blessings; in which he does not receive more than he deserves; in which, therefore, it becomes him to render thanks to the Providence that has made him what he is, and has given him what he has. And it is a fact that the most genuine praise and thanksgiving ascend from those hearts which in the eye of the world have the least to be thankful for. St. Paul chained to a soldier, and with the chains clanking upon his hands as he lifted them in adoration, cried to all suffering Christians: "Rejoice in the Lord; and again I say, rejoice." And this is true of nations as well as individuals. There is no people upon the earth, whatever may be their condition, who have not received from God infinitely beyond their deservings. He maketh his sun to shine upon the evil and the good, and sendeth his rain upon the just and the unjust, and therefore the gates of the temple of thanksgiving should never be shut, either in prosperity or adversity, either in peace or in war.

As a nation, we have certainly to be grateful for abundant harvests, for universal health, and for amicable relations with the other nations of the earth. These blessings were never more bountifully bestowed upon us than at this very moment. But we are at war among ourselves. Tens of thousands of our fellow-countrymen have been hurried to the judgment-seat of God; hundreds of thousands of hearts are bleeding for the loss of husbands, fathers, and sons; and millions of national wealth have been destroyed. What is there connected with this civil war in the United States of America that can possibly be matter of thankfulness? Is there any silver lining to this black cloud? That there is enough for fasting and humiliation in the present state of the country, none will dispute. But is there anything in the present contest that furnishes matter for devout and intelligent thanksgiving to Almighty God? We propose to answer this question. Fully alive to the evils of the war, and believing that it is one of those "offences" which our Lord affirms must "needs come" in a world of sinful and passionate men, and upon the authors of which he denounces a woe, we think, nevertheless, that there are some features and results of it for which it becomes all the loyal people of the land to be thankful. We believe that there are some characteristics in this contest which warrant every loyal American in saying: "The Lord is on my side; I will not fear: what can man do unto me? The Lord taketh my part with them that help me: therefore shall I see my desire upon them that hate me."

1. In the first place, we should give thanks to God, because *this war has been the occasion of deepening and strengthening the feeling of nationality.*

The relation of the individual to the State, of the American citizen to the American Union, never had a fuller or a deeper significance than now. The present civil war, and the existing struggle for national existence, throw a flood of light upon a class of truths which have been almost lost out of sight in the past years of peace, plenty, and increasing luxury. Since the war of independence by which we became a nation, and the naval war with England by which our nationality was made respectable before the world, the people of the United States have been too little tried by severe and sharp experiences for a solid and well-compacted growth. The nation has made too rapid territorial advance for the best prosperity, and the prophet Isaiah might say of us as he did of his own people: "Thou hast multiplied the nation, and not increased the joy." The same inexorable laws of national well-being have operated in our instance, as in that of ancient Rome. So long as the Roman could carry his nationality along with his conquests, so long as the energy of the Latin people was able to pervade the new elements that were received by the subjugation of provinces and could assimilate them—so long all was well. But when the bulk became too large to be thus permeated by the forces that issued from that wonderful nucleus of national life that was established on the Seven Hills by the union of the Latin with the Sabine blood; when the extent of conquered territory became so vast that it must be controlled and managed by standing armies, and so complex that it embraced all varieties of religion and civilization, then it fell apart by its own weight. While Rome was a monarchy and a republic she was a nation, and possessed a national life and strength. When she became an empire she lost her nationality, and her decline and fall came on apace.

Our nationality has not yet been destroyed, but it has been weakened by the operation of similar causes. We have added greatly to our territory, and not in every instance in that just and God-fearing manner in which the Pilgrims obtained possession of Massachusetts, and William Penn obtained Pennsylvania. The Old World has poured in upon us its hundreds of thousands.

This influx of foreign elements has been imperfectly assimilated, and, what is far worse, has been the occasion of engendering great political corruption by the continual endeavor of political parties to secure their weight and influence in the ever-recurring elections of the country. The original diversity of interests, occupations, and institutions, between the North and South, the two great halves of the one great whole, instead of disappearing, as was expected and desired by the fathers of the Constitution, became intense and exaggerated. Internal migration itself ran upon lines of latitude, and not in the least upon lines of longitude, so that the country presented to the eye of the foreign spectator two streams of population and of tendencies directly antagonistic, and which refusing to blend flowed side by side as the Ottawa flows beside the St. Lawrence. From these causes our nationality grew feebler from year to year, and was rapidly becoming, as one of the old grammarians remarks of the style of Seneca, "sand without lime." This imperfect consolidation of the federal government, and this growing diversity of feelings and interests between the two geographical sections, became the occasion of an open rupture and a civil war.

But that war has wakened anew the declining consciousness of nationality in the American people. It is the only unifying principle that now binds them together in their agony, and their victory. Destroy it, and the army breaks ranks immediately, and "resolves its mystic unity into the breathing atoms" that were gathered at the call of the bugle from the whole surface of the land. Destroy the sense of a national life, wider than that of the individual, and higher than that of any one of the single minor sovereignties that compose the American Union, and anarchy immediately begins. It is this simple, grand, master feeling that now overtops all others, and causes the American people, who are the most conflicting of any in their local views, and the most pertinacious of any in their private opinions, to present an undivided front and a solid column against treason and rebellion. Men of the most diverse social, political, and religious sentiments; men who differ greatly from one another respecting the causes of the rebellion; men who will be found to differ greatly from one another upon the grave and difficult questions that will arise when the rebellion is quelled, and the whole American people are once more assembled, by their representatives, in the national congress; men of all classes, conditions, and opinions have rallied with the unanimity of a single mind, and the determination of a single will, under that same flag that flung its rippling lines over the armies of Washington. They are fighting for the very same constitution, not altered in a single syllable, and never to be altered hereafter except by constitutional modes and methods, by which the original thirteen States became an organized nation, and into which all the rest have been grafted as living branches of the living vine.

This is something to be thankful for. It is a token of good from God, of favorable designs of the Supreme Arbiter, in relation to the country. For had he decreed to break it in pieces, he would not have wakened it to such a consciousness. He would have permitted the existing differences and dissensions, already many and great, to become distracting and dividing, and, as in the instance of the builders of Babel, would have prevented all unity and concert of action. But under his favoring providence, everything from the very opening of the war has conspired to widen, deepen, and strengthen the national sentiment and the national enthusiasm. It is stronger to-day than ever. The determination of the people at home, and the people in the camp, that "the Union must and shall be preserved," is now as firm and positive as it was in the will of that iron president who gave this motto to his countrymen. The maritime and manufacturing population of New England, the calm central masses of the Middle States, the prodigious energies of the West and Northwest, the gallantry and great self-sacrifice of the Border sovereignties, are all now massed and combined together as they never have been before. Could those two great statesmen who understood the genius of the American constitution better than any except its founders and framers, and whose eloquence from youth to old age was inspired by the idea of an *American nationality* more than by any other idea—could Webster and Clay revisit the earthly arena upon which they toiled and struggled, they would find that the master truth of their statesmanship and their oratory is now, at length, the dominant and living thought of the people. The masses have at last reached the height of their great argument; and that sentiment of Union for which they pleaded, and for which one of them lost his almost omnipotent local influence, while his name and his fame became all the more historic and universal, is now the sober and undying conviction of the day and the era.

2. In the second place, we should render profound and hearty thanks to Almighty God, on this day, because *the American Government is not waging an unjust war for foreign conquest, but a righteous war against domestic treason and rebellion.*

The demoralizing influence of national ambition, and of the wars that spring out of it, is universally conceded. When a nation is seized with the lust of conquest, and begins a military career for purposes of self-aggrandizement, the real patriot will weep bitterer tears over the fictitious and accursed glory that results, than over famine and pestilence. The American people within the past twenty years have shown some indications of such a temper, and had their career of prosperity been uninterrupted, it may have been that they would have formed no exception to the general rule that increase of power renders a nation arrogant, and would have fallen into the same class of examples with ancient Macedon and Rome, and modern Spain and France.

But as yet we have entered upon no such career of injustice and blood. On the contrary, we may hope that the present severe experience of the nation will exterminate all unlawful aspirations, and leave it sober, circumspect, and humble under the chastizing hand of God. This certainly is the tendency of the lesson of the hour; and if the people shall not thoroughly learn it; if, after they shall have emerged successfully from this intestine struggle, they shall seek collision with foreign nations, and aim at an empire to extend from the Great Bear to the Southern Cross, the vials of wrath will be poured out to their destruction and annihilation.

This is not a war for foreign conquest. It is a war against treason within the realm; as clearly so as those wars by which Great Britain has prevented Scotland and Ireland from becoming independent sovereignties, whenever factions and rebellions have been organized to accomplish this end. For the plea of the leaders of that alien government which has been constructed upon our southern borders, that they have the same right to demand and establish an independent existence, separate from the United States, that our common forefathers had when they achieved their independence, will not bear a moment's inspection. In the first place, the thirteen States which revolted against the government of Great Britain were distant colonies, separated from the mother country by three thousand miles of water; but the nine or ten States that have seceded from the American

Union without consulting the remaining partners in the compact,[1] are tied to the Union by geographical ligaments as close, strong, and vital as the spinal cord in the human frame. The original thirteen States, furthermore, constituted no portion of that European State-System of which Great Britain was an important member. Their career

[1] Even upon the theory of Calhoun that the Constitution is simply a *compact* between the States, the doctrine of the right of each State to be the sole judge of its grievances, and to secede from the Union at will, and by its own isolated action, is untenable. For a compact, when entered into, immediately changes the status and relations of the individual parties. It is a cession of a certain amount of personal sovereignty for value received, which amount of sovereignty cannot be resumed *without consent of parties*. A capitalist is not obliged to enter into partnership, but having voluntarily done so, he is no longer the entirely sovereign and independent person in respect to his capital, that he was before. He must hold it subject to the instrument or compact of partnership. In like manner, the State of South Carolina, e. g., upon entering into the Union, lost her status as a separate and independent sovereignty, because she solemnly bound herself to abide by the "constitutional compact" which she had voluntarily adopted, subject to revision and amendment by a majority of two-thirds of Congress, and three-fourths of the State legislatures. By adopting the Constitution, her condition and obligations became like those of a giver of a note or bond. The giving of the bond is optional; but *having been given*, its terms and promises must be kept.

Furthermore, the fact that a State must be *admitted* into the Union by a vote, proves that it cannot *leave* it but by a vote. It would be as absurd to allow Ohio to go out of the Union at will, and by its own isolated action, as it would have been to allow it to enter the Union in such a manner. The evils of permitting a person to join a mercantile partnership without the consent of the partners, would be no greater than those that would result from permitting him to leave it without such consent. Secession from the Union by independent State action, would justify accession to it by the same method. If mere self-will and self-interest, without

and their destiny would not sensibly affect the balance of power in the Old World, for they were out of all relations to it. But the States of Virginia and Louisiana, by their geography, are as intimately identified with the American Union, are as inextricably involved in it, as the counties of Middlesex and York are with the three kingdoms that constitute Great Britain. It was one thing for thirteen distant colonies to declare their independence of the British empire, and a very different thing for an English county to do this. A new nation might spring into being three thousand miles from the island of Great Britain, without danger either to the British constitution, or to the system of European States, and, as it turned out, with great benefit to them both; but a new and alien government, constituted out of an organic and integral part of the very island itself, would have been the annihilation of the English power and the English realm.

But again, the alleged parallelism between the two instances fails in another most important particular. The thirteen colonies were not equal members of a democratic republic, but inferior dependencies upon a monarchy flushed with power,

any regard to the will and vote of the constituted majority, may rule in the former instance, why not in the latter? Says Madison: "It surely does not follow from the fact that the States, *or rather the people embodied in them*, have, as parties to the constitutional compact, no tribunal above them, that in controverted meanings of the compact, a *minority* of the parties can rightfully decide against the *majority;* still less that a *single party* can at will *withdraw itself altogether from its compact with the rest.*"

and fenced with the descending orders of nobility. They revolted from the mother country simply and solely because they had no representation upon the floor of the British parliament. It was not the tax upon tea, it was not the stamp act, it was not any very great aversion to a monarchical form of government, as such, that fired the heart of our Revolutionary fathers. The statement of Webster is strictly true: "They went to war against a preamble. They fought seven years against a declaration." In the phraseology of the most beautiful and magnificent period that ever dropped from those charmed lips: "On a question of *principle*, while actual suffering was yet afar off, they raised their flag against a power, to which, for purposes of foreign conquest and subjugation, Rome, in the height of her glory, is not to be compared; a power which has dotted over the surface of the whole globe with her possessions and military posts, whose morning drum-beat following the sun, and keeping company with the hours, circles the earth daily with one continuous and unbroken strain of the martial airs of England." It was simply the refusal to place the people of the colonies upon the *same footing* with the people of the mother country—giving them the same constitutional rights and privileges, no more and no less—that led our forefathers to throw off their allegiance, and establish an independent government. Had this reasonable demand been conceded, the brightest of its jewels, perhaps, might not have dropped from the English crown, and to this day we might have been Englishmen under a hereditary monarchy, and as proud of the rich and glorious history of England as we now are of our own brilliant and striking career. The wise men of that time, the Burkes and the Chathams, knew this, and saw this; but the wisdom of these statesmen was overborne by the folly of those politicians who happened, as it has happened since, to be in the ascendant at a critical instant. The people of the seceding States can make no such complaint as this. They were not colonies and dependencies of a monarchical Empire. They were members of a democratic Union. They had an equal, and in one particular, a superior representation in the national Congress with those States whom they now charge with being their tyrants and their invaders, and whom they would compare with that aristocratic and arbitrary parliament that denied to Massachusetts and South Carolina any participation in the common deliberations and decisions of the British realm.

In these two facts, then, namely: that the Confederate States are as geographically connected with the American Union as an English county is with the island of Great Britain, and that they have a common representation and vote in the national councils, we find the proof that this war has no analogy with that by which our fathers gained their independence, but is simply a domestic rebellion upon one side, and the exertion of constitutional power upon the other. The United States of America are engaged in suppressing the treason of a portion of the population, and defeating their attempt to overthrow the common government. There is no intention of depriving any loyal state, or any loyal citizen, of a single iota of his constitutional rights. It is a war to maintain a common constitution and preserve a democratic government.[1]

And at this point another fact stares us in the face that goes to strengthen the positions that have been taken, and to prove still more convincingly that this war is a righteous one upon the side of the Government, and a wrong one upon that of its enemies. There is no necessity of redressing

[1] The declarations of the President and Congress of the United States, prove this assertion. The Inaugural Address of President Lincoln contained the following passage: "Apprehension seems to exist among the people of the Southern States, that by the accession of a Republican Administration, their property, and their peace and personal security are to be endangered. There has never been any reasonable cause for such apprehension. Indeed, the most ample evidence to the contrary has all the while existed and been open to their inspection. It is found in nearly all the published speeches of him who now addresses you. I do but quote from one of those speeches when I declare that ' I have no purpose, directly or indirectly, to interfere with the institution of slavery in the States where it exists. I believe I have no lawful right to do so, and I have no inclination to do so.' Those who nominated and elected me, did so with a full knowledge that I had made this and many other similar declarations, and had never recanted them." And the last Congress passed the following resolution of Mr. Crittenden, affirming: "That this war is not waged in any spirit of oppression, or for any purpose of conquest or subjugation, or purpose of overthrowing, or interfering with the rights or established institutions of any State, but to defend and maintain the supremacy of the Constitution, and to preserve the Union, with all the dignity, equality, and rights of the several States unimpaired, and that as soon as these objects are accomplished, the war ought to cease."

grievances, either real or imaginary, under a democratic government, by the awful method of war. *The right of armed revolution does not hold good in a democracy.* When a people are governing themselves by universal suffrage; when no portion of them is made inferior by the law and constitution of the land to any other portion; when neither birth, nor wealth, nor even education and religion, give any superior political power or privilege to a class or a section, it is the sheerest self-will and the worst of crimes, for a portion of the people to plunge the whole land into the horrors of war, for the removal of either real or imaginary grievances. If the political constitution of a country gives certain political rights to some of the citizens or some of the sections, and denies them to the remainder; if the citizens or the sections are not equal in the eye of the organic law of the realm; then the right of armed revolution is a valid one. For then there is no mode of redressing grievances, in the last resort, but by war. It cannot be done by universal and equal suffrage, and therefore it must be done by gunpowder and cannon. The axiom that armed revolution is justifiable has grown up in the Old World, which is a world of unequal rights, a world of aristocracies, of monarchies, and of despotisms, and it is undoubtedly true there; but when it travels across the Atlantic, and comes into a new world of democratic ideas, and purely representative sovereignties, and universal suffrage, it ceases to be true; it is no longer an axiom.

For even if a majority should prove tyrannical, and trample on the vested rights of a minority, their triumph can be only *temporary*. It is not supposable that from year to year, and from one generation to another, the preponderance will continue to be upon the side of injustice and wrong, in a country where universal suffrage prevails. Even when no critical questions are to be decided, even in the ordinary politics of popular government, the triumph is continually oscillating from one side to the other. No majority maintains itself as such from generation to generation. One administration goes and another comes, but the republic abides continually. Much less will a majority continue to hold power from year to year, when its victory is founded on a breach of constitutional rights, and results in tyranny and injustice toward the minority of the nation. It is therefore always the duty of the lesser portion to wait calmly for the sober second thought of the nation of which it is an integral part. The resort to the horrors of war can never be justified under a republican government, where the will of the people, and not the power of a king, and peerage, and privileged classes, is the sovereign arbiter. The Southern States of the American Union needed only to bide their time, to enjoy their entire constitutional and vested rights. We say this the more readily, because, though we cannot concede the reality of all their alleged grievances, we nevertheless sympathized deeply, and still sympathize, with that portion of the people who believe that the American Constitution is a compromise between opposing views, and that the true politics for the whole nation lies in that general line of direction. But the reckless rush to arms for the redress of grievances; the repudiation of the national symbol; the erection of another government in the very heart of the land, and the gathering of armies to uphold it; all this immediately made it the first and only duty of every patriot to put down domestic treason, and again lift up the national flag where it had been struck down.

But if the unrighteousness of this armed rebellion of the Southern States is clearly evident from the position of democracy, it is still more so from that of Christianity. It cannot be justified on the principles of the gospel. Were the rights of conscience involved, and were there no peaceable mode of securing them through the ballot-box; were it an instance in which a Phillip II. were attempting to force the doctrines of the Papacy upon a Protestant province and dependency: then armed resistance would not only be allowable, but it would be blessed and crowned with glory and immortality, by the Lord and Head of the Church himself. In such a case, he says to his servants: " He that hath no sword, let him sell his garment and buy one." But the rights of conscience are not touched in the least, in this conflict. The questions that are involved are purely political, certainly so far as the aims of the leaders of the rebellion are concerned. It will not be pretended that they have plunged the whole country into war for the purpose of improving the moral and religious condition of the Southern people, and of the four millions of slaves who are in bondage to them. It is true that the wrath of man will praise God in this as in every instance, and this war will undoubtedly result in moral and religious benefit to the Northern and Southern citizen, and to the Southern slave, but so far as the purposes of the Confederate politicians are concerned, it is a purely political war, and stands in no connection with either ethics or Christianity. It is not even a struggle for personal liberty, which, in the eye of Christianity, is a matter of secondary importance, provided the soul can enjoy "the liberty wherewith Christ maketh free."

Even if the South had been despoiled of certain democratic rights and privileges, St. Paul might say to them, as he said to the Christian bondman as he sat with his master at the table of the Lord, and looked forward to a higher citizenship than that of earth: "Art thou called being a servant? *Care not for it.*" Rights and privileges that appear of highest importance from a political point of view, sometimes become of secondary consequence from the Christian position; and a war that would be justified by the principles of mere democracy, might be condemned altogether by the precepts of the gospel. And it is precisely here, that we affirm, with all confidence, that the attitude of the Southern Church has been wrong. Knowing the principles by which the proud natural man is actuated, we could not expect that the passionate and imperious Southron would turn the left cheek, in case he had been smitten upon the right. We do not expect, in the history of the world, that unregenerate human nature will be actuated by those meek and forgiving sentiments that belong to the children of God. But we had a right to expect that the Church of Christ in the Southern States would not be in the van of the rebellion; that their heavenly charity would suffer long, bearing all things, hoping all things, and enduring all things. Even accepting the Southern judgment respecting the points in dispute, and the Southern estimate of grievances, it still remains true that the principles of the gospel forbade the employment of "wars and fightings" to settle them. If a disciple of Christ meets even with insult and abuse in the streets of Charleston, or of New York, his religion forbids him to render railing for railing, or to return blow for blow. Except in the extreme instance of saving his very life itself, he is prohibited from shedding human blood, and taking human life. The same principle applies to war, and the relation which the Church should sustain to it. But we have showed that no such *dire necessity* of war overhung the democratic institutions and democratic populations of either South or North; and therefore it follows that when the Southern Church descended from its high position above the passions of the world, and trailed its white robes in that secular and unhallowed procession which kindled the fires of intestine and fratricidal war, it committed a sin. Instead of feeding the passions of the high-strung, chivalrous, but ambitious and unregenerate masses amidst whom it had been planted, the Southern Church ought to have allayed them. She ought to have stood firm upon the position of the gospel, and to have cried with clear commanding voice to the multitude and their leaders: "Forgive your enemies; if thine enemy hunger, feed him; if he thirst, give him drink. From whence come wars and fightings among you? come they not hence, even of your lusts that war in your members? Ye lust and have not: ye kill and desire to have, and cannot obtain: ye fight and war, yet ye have not, *because ye ask not.*" It was the method of peace, of forbearance, and of charity, that should have been urged by the Christians of the South in that time when madness ruled the hour; and for this method, if need be, they ought even to have dared to die. And had there been this Christian daring, the reward might have been that civic garland which is hung upon the brow of him who gains the victories of peace, which are greater than the victories of war. The judgment that issued from this pulpit one year ago, from lips and wisdom that have done much to guide the councils of a Church that is second to none in weight and influence through the land, is undoubtedly true: "A little firmness on the part of our Southern brethren would have chained the dogs of war, and saved the country."[1]

[1] The reference is to Gardiner Spring, D.D.

3. In the third place, *the judgment and attitude of the American people and government, during this civil war, respecting the system of slavery*, is a reason for thanksgiving to God. Upon this difficult and exciting subject they have avoided the two extremes into which particular parties, both in this country and abroad, have fallen. In the first place, the mass of the nation and their rulers have rejected with an instantaneous decision the doctrine that slavery is right and righteous in itself. They deny that it stands upon the same basis with the institutions of the family, the state, and the church. The doctrine that human bondage is ordained of God, and founded in natural right, has obtained no advocates among those to whom the guidance of our national affairs has been committed. Upon this point, the mass of the people and their rulers stand with the fathers and framers of the Constitution; our enemies themselves being judges. For it is the declaration of the vice-president of the Southern Confederacy, that the lapse of time and further illumination have enabled the architects of the new political structure to correct the judgment of our common ancestors upon the subject of slavery. The position which the American people and their government have taken before God and the world is, that the system of human bondage is intrinsically an unjust one; that it could not exist in a perfect world; and that the progress of Christianity will invariably destroy it wherever it exists. This of itself proves that it has no foundation in the ordi-

nance of God, or in the natural rights which he has established. The Christian religion will root up no plant which the Heavenly Father has planted. Whatever is abstractly right and righteous, whatever is ordained of God, will live through the millennium, and to the great burning day.

But, on the other hand, the American people and government have not been able to see that an instantaneous emancipation of the four millions in bondage would be best either for them, or for the nation with whose weal and woe they are connected. On the contrary, they look to a gradual method that shall prepare them for freedom and self-government. They desire that slavery should be removed at the South, as it was at the North, by the voluntary action of the States themselves. A compulsory reform, even if it is possible, is undesirable. The slave-owner must himself, of his own free will, manumit his bondmen. And it is in this reference that the maintenance of the American Union is of untold importance. The future welfare of the black man, as well as the white man, depends upon the perpetuity of the *United* States of America. In the three quarters of a century during which the evil of slavery has existed under the American constitution, a process of amelioration has been going on, which if unchecked will secure its final removal. It required several centuries to eradicate human bondage from the ancient Christendom ; but fifty years more of such influences and tendencies as were at work when the North and the South met in a harmonious congress, and the great questions of the country were discussed in a comprehensive and national style and temper, would result in the substantial emancipation of the African race. This happy consummation now depends upon the restoration of the Union. If the country is dismembered, and a Southern Confederacy is established, the future of the slave is overhung with black darkness. But if the North and the South shall be again united upon the ancient constitutional basis, the Federal Government being acknowledged as supreme within its sphere, while yet the rights reserved to the several States are not infringed upon in the least, then "the era of good feeling" will dawn once more, the difficult problems will be examined in that conciliatory temper which characterized the discussions that accompanied the formation and adoption of the Constitution, and a way of escape out of his bondage will be discovered for the African, that will cause no exasperation, and shed no human blood.

It is matter of devout thanksgiving to God, in whose hand are the hearts of all men, that the American people and government are standing upon this position. Thomas Jefferson, after describing the evil nature and influence of the system of human bondage, enforces all that he has advanced upon this point, by the remark, "I tremble for my country when I remember that God is just." Well might every American tremble for the result of this civil war, if the people and government stood before God and the world, as do the leaders of the Southern rebellion, affirming the inherent righteousness of human bondage, and laying it down as the corner stone of a political edifice. But they are no such advocates of a system which has been condemned and rejected by all the other civilized nations of the world, and upon which the frown of Divine Providence manifestly rests. They desire its removal, they look for its removal, and they are ready to pour out their treasure without stint to accomplish it. At the same time they remember that it is not like an individual sin, which because it is confined to a single person can be put away by a volition. It is an hereditary corruption, organized into human societies and relationships, which it requires time and persevering effort perfectly to eradicate. They also bear in mind that the States most directly concerned should have a voice in respect to the ways and the means, should come into the common councils of the nation and deliberate, and should legislate upon it precisely as did the States of New York and Massachusetts when they put away the evil from among them.

Such, then, are some of the reasons for thanksgiving in this time of rebellion and civil war. Such are some of the grounds for hoping and believing that that Supreme Arbiter who sets up and pulls down the nations of the earth as it pleases him, is upon the side of the American people and government in their endeavor to prevent a dissolution of their Union, and the long-continued wars and anarchy that must result from such a catastrophe. The consciousness that we are and must continue to be one nation and people, has been evoked and strengthened by the conflict. Our armies are not seeking to conquer any foreign country, but simply to preserve the boundaries of the United States intact. They are battling solely to maintain the authority of the Constitution—an instrument of remarkable political wisdom, well adapted to secure the interests of all sections of the land, and under whose benign influences all sections have enjoyed a singular peace and prosperity for seventy-five years. And, lastly, they are not fighting to perpetuate forever the system of human slavery, but to preserve a government and an order of things under which that system has been gradually waning in power and influence, and through which alone it can be ultimately abolished.

If these things are so, if we have not erred in our judgment, may not every loyal American take up, humbly yet confidently, the utterance of the Psalmist: "The Lord is on my side; I will not fear: what can man do unto me? The Lord taketh my part with them that help me; therefore shall I see my desire upon them that hate me." While the people and their rulers ought to humble themselves under the mighty hand of God, for the pride, the vain-glory, and the self-confidence which have brought these terrible judgments upon them, we verily think that they should give thanks to God, that so far as the *principles* that underlie this civil war are concerned, they are in the right, and their opponents are in the wrong. We believe that the time will come when our Southern fellow-countrymen will see that this rebellion was needless, was reckless, was unrighteous; that the Constitution which their fathers adopted, and to which they themselves had sworn allegiance, had power and virtue enough in it to secure the rights of all sections of the nation; and that they needed only to bide their time, and give it a full trial, to find it what Washington denominated it, "the palladium of their political safety and prosperity." We believe that the time is coming, when the sentiments of the Father of his country, enunciated in his "Farewell Address," respecting the *sacredness of the Constitution*, and the obligation of all the people to respect its provisions, will be read in the light of this rebellion with calm joy by those who have stood by the Union, and with sorrow by those who have struck at its life. "The Constitution," says Washington, "which at any time exists, *till changed by an explicit act of the whole people, is sacredly obligatory upon all.*"

Confessing with deep humility our national sins, we may nevertheless be thankful, upon this day, that our national attitude in the war is what it is. Through the thick cloud that envelops the present, we may look for a brighter future. We expect the perpetuity of the American Union. We expect the return of the seceding States upon the ancient basis, and with the old national feeling. There will be deep joy and thanksgiving, but there will be no *triumph* over the result. It will be Americans meeting Americans after a temporary alienation. It was a law in the Roman state that the general who had been victorious in a *civil* war should enjoy no triumph. It was only when the struggle had been with a foreign enemy, and the Roman arms had been successful, that the Imperator returned to the city in his triumphal chariot, followed by his soldiers and the long line of captives and spoils. But when the contest had been between Roman and Roman; when the state had succeeded in quelling an intestine rebellion, or settling an internal dissension; the successful general found his triumph in his success and the private regard of the citizens. Antony celebrated no triumph even upon the suppression of the conspiracy of Catiline; Cinna and Marius arrogated to themselves no public honors for their victory over the party of Sulla; and Julius Cæsar, after the memorable battle of Pharsalia, did not lead the remnants of the great party of Pompey in chains up the Capitolian Hill. A civil war is too sad, and too exhausting, to be followed by triumphal processions.

In this spirit let the war be prosecuted. Let it be confined strictly to the restoration of the authority of the Constitution over all parts of the land. Let it be understood that the questions in dispute between the North and the South may and can be settled by the old constitutional and peaceful methods of public discussion and the ballot-box; but that their settlement by armed revolution, by the dismemberment of the American Union, and by the establishment of another government upon the southern borders of the land, is impossible. Right, and justice, and moderation will then be the strength of our cause. With all our sin and unworthiness, we can nevertheless appeal to the God of battles that our motives in this war are upright, and that our success will be a blessing to the entire nation, South as well as North. Then may we lift up in thanksgiving that lowly, and that lofty psalm: "If it had not been the Lord who was on our side, now may Israel say; if it had not been the Lord who was on our side, when men rose up against us; then had they swallowed us up quick, when their wrath was kindled against us; then the waters had overwhelmed us, the stream had gone over our soul; then the proud waters had gone over our soul. Blessed be the Lord, who hath not given us a prey to their teeth. Our soul is escaped as a bird out of the snare of the fowlers; the snare is broken, and we are escaped. Our help is in the name of the Lord, who made heaven and earth."

OTHER SHEDD TITLES FROM SOLID GROUND

Solid Ground Christian Books is delighted to have the following books now in print from W.G.T. Shedd –

Sermons to the Natural Man – In the words of A.A. Hodge: "Dr. Shedd's *Sermons to the Natural Man* are, if not absolutely the best, yet of the very best doctrinal and spiritual sermons produced in this generation. We have known much of their power in convincing sinners, and in deepening, widening and exalting the experience of true Christians."

Sermons to the Spiritual Man – "This volume is complementary to another, published in 1871, under the title of *Sermons to the Natural Man*. In the earlier volume, the author aimed to address the human conscience. In this, he would speak to the Christian heart. The former supposed original and unpardoned sin, and endeavored to produce the consciousness of it. The latter supposes forgiven and indwelling sin, and would aid in the struggle and victory over it."

Homiletics and Pastoral Theology – Dr. W.G.T. Shedd expounds almost every aspect of preaching, analyzing its nature, outlining the main features which should characterize powerful preaching and describing the approach, plan, actual construction and refinements of a sermon. This volume was used for many years as a standard textbook in several theological seminaries throughout the United States.

The History of Christian Doctrine – "I have often referred to Shedd's *History of Christian Doctrine* in preparation for class, for personal understanding of difficult issues, and for solid evangelical encouragement." - Dr. Tom J. Nettles

Call us at 205-443-0311
Send us an e-mail at sgcb@charter.net
Visit us on the web at solid-ground-books.com

www.ingramcontent.com/pod-product-compliance
Lightning Source LLC
Chambersburg PA
CBHW022051160426
43198CB00008B/197